Trauma-Sensitive Literacy Instruction

Trauma-Sensitive Literacy Instruction

Building Student Resilience in English-Language Arts Classrooms

Rachelle S. Savitz and Britnie Delinger Kane

Foreword by Elizabeth Dutro

TEACHERS COLLEGE PRESS
TEACHERS COLLEGE | COLUMBIA UNIVERSITY
NEW YORK AND LONDON

Published by Teachers College Press,® 1234 Amsterdam Avenue, New York, NY 10027

Front cover image by Bill Tyne via Flickr Creative Commons.

Library of Congress Cataloging-in-Publication Data

Names: Savitz, Rachelle S., author. | Kane, Britnie Delinger, author.
Title: Trauma-sensitive literacy instruction : building student resilience in English-language arts classrooms / Rachelle S. Savitz and Britnie Delinger Kane ; foreword by Elizabeth Dutro.
Description: New York : Teachers College Press, [2023] | Includes bibliographical references and index.
Identifiers: LCCN 2023004093 (print) | LCCN 2023004094 (ebook) | ISBN 9780807768921 (paper : acid-free paper) | ISBN 9780807768938 (hardcover : acid-free paper) | ISBN 9780807782019 (ebook)
Subjects: LCSH: Children with mental disabilities—Education. | Psychic trauma in children. | Post-traumatic stress disorder in children. | Language arts. | English language—Study and teaching—Social aspects. | Minorities in literature. | Creative teaching. | Teacher-student relationships.
Classification: LCC LC4165 .S28 2023 (print) | LCC LC4165 (ebook) | DDC 371.94—dc23/eng/20230329
LC record available at https://lccn.loc.gov/2023004093
LC ebook record available at https://lccn.loc.gov/2023004094

ISBN 978-0-8077-6892-1 (paper)
ISBN 978-0-8077-6893-8 (hardcover)
ISBN 978-0-8077-8201-9 (ebook)

Printed on acid-free paper
Manufactured in the United States of America

This book is lovingly dedicated to Erika Savitz and the Savitz family for their love and support.

—R.S.S.

To my family—Ian, Maren, Sawyer, and Griffin—for understanding why Mom needed to stay late (again) to get this writing done, and to my sister, for sharing her wisdom as a teacher, a mother, and a friend. Without each of you, my life would be less.

—B.D.K.

Contents

Foreword

My reading of Savitz and Kane's timely and beautifully written book corresponded with my rereading of some of my favorite writing by bell hooks, the brilliant Black feminist writer, scholar, and philosopher, whose untimely passing in 2021 left so many reaching for her words, her legacy. Perhaps it is the intertwining of those texts that explains why I found myself contemplating the idea of *presence* as I sat down to write this foreword. Presence, in its multiple facets, runs through Savitz and Kane's discussions of teaching that honors and supports students in the face of trauma. And the importance of presence consistently shines as a theme in hooks's writing, particularly her writing about pedagogy. hooks writes that "any radical pedagogy must insist that everyone's presence is acknowledged. That insistence cannot be simply stated. It has to be demonstrated through pedagogical practices" (2014, p. 8). Why this quote, in this foreword, to this book? Because, let's be clear, to teach in ways that are responsive to the presence of multiple dimensions of students' lives, including the hardest things—and to be present for and with students in compassion, love, and fierce advocacy and solidarity—*is* radical pedagogy. It is the brave, persistent, justice-fueled pedagogy necessary, now and always, to honor and include all that life infuses into schools, and all the more so when lived experience encounters the texts and expressive tools of English Language Arts classrooms. In this book, ELA teachers will find actionable pedagogical practices toward the transformative teaching trauma demands and the respect, care, and support along the way that ELA educators need and deserve.

To dwell in that idea of presence and why it was resonant for me as I read across these chapters, here are just some of the ways I see Savitz and Kane capturing what *is* present and how to *be* present in the midst of the personal, societal, and institutional traumas students and teachers experience.

Presence of trauma, as a given in ELA classrooms. These authors remind us that trauma is always in the classroom. As teachers, we do not need to ask if difficult experiences are present. The fragility of human life, the certainty of institutional racism, transphobia, and other systemic oppressions, and the violence within and outside of schools is all the evidence we need. Instead, we must embrace pedagogies that recognize trauma, honor the knowledge born from trauma, challenge pathologizing narratives that attention to trauma can fuel, gather the resources necessary, and link arms with other educators to confront the fears and uncertainties that may forestall action.

Presence of justice as the central goal in trauma-sensitive ELA teaching. Savitz and Kane place justice at the heart of their book. Like many other educators who have witnessed the recent wave of attention to trauma-informed education and the very different forms it can take, I have no patience for approaches to trauma in schools that fail to center equity and justice. Educators need resources, like this book and others these authors provide, that put actions to words and support educators to reckon with how attention to trauma can create or exacerbate the trauma that schools inflict on students, particularly BIPOC and LGBTQ+ youth.

Presence of joy and brilliance, always. In these pages, educators will find consistent reminders of the crucial idea that students are always demonstrating the importance of recognizing how the joys of life and the vibrancy of youth's knowledge and identities flourish alongside the challenges that they navigate. Trauma-sensitive teaching *requires* recognizing joy and brilliance.

Presence of students. Students are tangibly present in these pages. The authors' story-centered writing ensures readers will feel connected to multifaceted young people. Throughout, Savitz and Kane emphasize the presence of students' lived knowledge, their capacities for empathic presence with others, and their right to agential responses to intentionally crafted invitations to bring their lives to school literacies. A term like "resilience" is not stable, nor unitary, in its meaning and implications, as it is only helpful when it holds full recognition of the already-present, powerful resilience that many students draw upon to survive and attempt to thrive amidst the institutional and societal oppressions in schools and society. ELA educators can reframe "resilience" in light of the varying and multiple dimensions trauma takes in students' lives. This book provides actionable strategies for teachers to consider the range of visible and too-often-overlooked ways that students are present in ELA classrooms.

Presence of teachers. Savitz and Kane's identities as teachers fuel each chapter of this book. They delve into the layers of presence that trauma demands from educators and, importantly, the presence of teachers' lives, humanity, and needs for tangible support and solidarity. The authors write with deep compassion for educators who are navigating students' well-being, while trying not to lose sight of their own.

Hard things are present in the lives of students and teachers, always. This book, however, is arriving at a time when those educators reaching for it may feel particularly inundated by trauma: the loss and grief of the COVID-19 pandemic; continual horrors of gun violence in neighborhoods, communities, and, far too often, schools; accelerations of overt hate speech and actions; the judicial stripping away of rights to bodily autonomy and hateful state legislation targeting trans youth and queer communities; and seeking to expel the truths of history and experience of BIPOC from schools. All of it fuels the sense of trauma's relentlessness. What this book makes clear and helps to make possible is to see trauma's presence as a call to action to be with others in the challenges—with students, with other educators—"to hear each other (the sound of different voices), to listen to one another, [as] an exercise in recognition" (hooks, 2014, p. 41). We can recognize that ELA classrooms can hold all of the stories students and teachers have lived and invite the fullness of life to infuse school literacies with vibrancy, care, hope, and commitment. If they don't, we have to do better. This book can help.

—Elizabeth Dutro
University of Colorado Boulder
December 2022

REFERENCE

hooks, b. (2014). *Teaching to transgress*. Routledge.

Acknowledgments

We have been inspired by many educators and teacher educators who incorporate trauma-sensitive literacy instruction (TSLI) into their classrooms. We have also been inspired by our colleagues who have crossed our paths, questioned our perspectives, and supported our thoughts as we connected their work with that of other greats in our field. With them, this work is possible. We are grateful for learning alongside so many people we have met at conferences, through organizations, and at work. Thank you, East Carolina University and The Citadel.

We want to thank Drs. Douglas Fisher and Nancy Frey, with whom I (Rachelle) coauthored *Teaching Hope and Resilience for Students Experiencing Trauma: Creating Safe and Nurturing Classrooms for Learning*. Without Doug and Nancy, this book would have been impossible. Their mentorship and guidance about writing a book were invaluable; their experience and expertise in trauma-sensitive instruction and resilience strengthened my stance on this pedagogical practice. Without writing this book together, I (Rachelle) would have never dreamed of exploring a second book that follows up on ideas and thoughts shared in our first book.

We are also grateful for the many teachers, administrators, school officials, and teacher educators who have shared their voices and classrooms with our readers and us. In particular, we would like to thank Brooke Bianchi-Pennington, Lindsey Blustein, Rachel Bolte, Jason DeHart, Steven Jernigan, April Leach, Rachel Long, Katie McGee, Carmen Marroquin, Jennifer Morrison, Debbie Myers, Darius Phelps, Stacey Reece, Lesley Roessing, Taylor Simmons, and Emma Willard for contributing their time and talents as they wrote the vignettes that enrich the pages of this book. We value learning with and from others and know that a book written from our experiences alone would not have been the same. We recognize the value of your rich contributions. Your knowledge and love formed after years of experience and dedication in classrooms are noted and appreciated by all.

We want to shout out to our biological and chosen family and friends. Thank you for listening as we talked through ideas, problem-solved writing blocks, and stressed over what we couldn't figure out was missing—until our conversations. We are grateful for your support in providing us time to write, reflect, create, and think, continuously encouraging us not to give up. Dr. Amy Broemmel and Dr. Jacy Ippolito, thank you.

We also want to thank Mrs. Charlene Aldrich and Mrs. Katie McGee. They provided outstanding editorial assistance and new ways to think through what we wanted to share with our readers. We appreciate your expert attention to detail and advice along the way.

We would also like to thank Dr. Elizabeth Dutro, who has influenced our work and this book in many ways. We thank her for writing our foreward and seeing the potential and intentions of our book to provide ELA teachers with applicable trauma-sensitive practices and pedagogies.

Finally, we would like to thank Emily Spangler and Regina Ward from Teachers College Press, who were excited about this second book and encouraged and guided us along the way. Thank you for appreciating and understanding how we approached TSLI.

CHAPTER 1

Introduction

In the middle of teaching class one day, I (Rachelle) received a text message from Haisley (pseudonym), a student who had been absent that morning. The message would have seemed fairly innocuous to most people, but—to me—it was clear something was wrong. Haisley's text message thanked me for being supportive and for always being there for her. While her communications in the past had been similar, the way she wrote this sounded more final. I knew immediately that I needed to do something. After a few grueling minutes, I found an administrator to cover my classroom while I reached out first to Haisley and then, when Haisley didn't answer, to her mother. Within minutes, an ambulance arrived at her house, as Haisley had attempted to take her own life and was minutes away from detrimental consequences.

Haisley was dealing with extreme bullying in and out of school; she was fearful of walking from the bus to her house. Importantly, I understood that Haisley was not okay, and—although she did not use those words—her text message was a critical warning sign to "come quick." I received her unspoken message only because of the trusting relationship she and I had developed.

Sadly, in my 15 years working in public education, Haisley was not the only student who reached out to me for a lifeline. In this case, she reached out using a text message. You may not choose to text with your students (more on that later), but you likely know students—like Haisley—who are experiencing trauma. What you may not know is how prevalent students' experiences of trauma really are.

Trauma is not the exception in middle and high schools in the United States—it is the rule. According to Briere and Scott (2015), trauma is any event that is "extremely upsetting, at least temporarily overwhelms an individual's internal resources, and produces lasting psychological symptoms" (p. 10). Trauma can cause physical, emotional, and life-threatening harm and have lasting adverse effects on the individual's mental, physical, and emotional health.

The National Traumatic Stress Network (n.d.) has identified more categories of trauma in childhood than there are in adulthood, including the following 12 types related to children: bullying, community violence, complex trauma, disasters (i.e., natural or related to war), early childhood trauma, intimate partner violence of a family member or themselves, medical trauma, physical abuse, refugee trauma, sexual abuse, terrorism and violence, and traumatic grief. These traumatic experiences are commonly referred to as adverse childhood experiences (ACEs). According to the 2017–2018 National Survey of Children's Health (2019), one of every three children between birth and age 17 had at least one ACE, and 14.1% had two or more ACEs in the past year.

It is also important to note that children's experiences of trauma are frequently distributed inequitably: The National Survey of Children's Health reported that 22% percent of children whose family income falls below the federal poverty level experienced two or more ACEs, whereas only 7.3% of children whose family income is four times the federal poverty level experienced two or more ACEs. Race is also a variable, with a larger percentage of non-Hispanic Black children experiencing two or more ACEs compared to non-Hispanic white children (21.3% vs. 12.9%). As Craig (2017) states, "those marginalized by race, sexual orientation, disability, poverty, or immigration status" are especially vulnerable (p. 5). Sadly, these statistics highlight the pervasiveness of trauma in children's and adolescents' lives.

The most common trauma experienced by children and adolescents includes chronic and/or systemic acts of violence that repeatedly occur within the home or community (Meyers, 2014). Rumsey and colleagues (2020) found that the most frequent types of trauma reported by 361 school counselors were "major upheaval between parents, including domestic violence, separation, and divorce; the death of a close friend or family member; and emotional abuse," and more of these types of trauma were reported to have occurred in Title I schools (p. 7). This is important for educators to know and understand because, as children experience trauma, they often have feelings of powerlessness, asking, "Why me?" Indeed, environments that take away a child's sense of stability or safety can lead to traumatic experiences. Feelings of powerlessness are often accompanied by feelings of shame, humiliation, or betrayal and a "concern that adults will think less of them" if they disclose what happened (Craig, 2017, p. 48).

Despite the disheartening normalcy of trauma, teachers may not know how to recognize or respond to a student's traumatic experiences. Indeed, because teachers often feel ill-equipped to deal with students' experiences of trauma, they may steer clear of these socially and interpersonally tricky conversations. However, there is a tremendous educational cost to doing so, and the price is both intellectual and emotional. For over 50 years, the research on high-quality instruction that reaches *every* student has highlighted that—if we are to support students' access to rigorous academic ideas—we must ensure that students' perspectives and life experiences are not an add-on to curricula but a central part of it (e.g., Ladson-Billings, 1995; Paris, 2012). If students' life experiences include trauma—which they do far more often than is comfortable to admit—teachers must learn how to incorporate trauma-sensitive instructional practices into their daily work.

Of course, teachers don't leave discussions of trauma out of the classroom because they want students to feel ashamed. They usually do it because they don't feel confident they can support students with these difficulties. Teachers fear they are not mental health counselors and will cause additional harm; these are serious concerns. The following chapters will address how to set boundaries when consulting with parents, guardians, school counselors, and administrators, and the importance of knowing additional community resources and local mental health agencies (Craig, 2008). While acknowledging the seriousness of supporting students who experience trauma, we also recognize the severity of ignoring students' experiences of trauma, which may continue the harm many students are already experiencing.

Fortunately, over the past few years, research on socio-emotional learning (SEL) has become more common, and teachers discuss trauma more frequently. This is important since so many of our students are experiencing trauma. However, when we visit schools, we see that many teachers attempt to support these students by adopting stand-alone programming or devoting 45 minutes or so a week to SEL. Yet, we know that the most effective way to support students experiencing trauma is to embed support for SEL within classroom instruction.

Trauma-sensitive instructional practices place students' experiences—all of their experiences, even the traumatic ones—firmly within the confines of the English Language Arts curriculum. If you feel a knot forming in your stomach right now, you should. Such work can be scary and uncomfortable. Often, trauma-related topics are considered taboo and left out of the curriculum. In this way, students experiencing trauma are asked to leave their genuine worries, concerns, and fears at the door. They are asked to focus strictly on what is taught—*Julius Caesar* or *Of Mice and Men*. Sadly, when students' lives are left out of these discussions, it heightens the belief that what a student is experiencing is not okay. Shame replaces resilience. Yet it need not be this way. Research highlights that trauma-sensitive instructional practices can support students' achievement and promote students' resilience—the ability to recover or adapt to complex challenges (Fisher et al., 2020).

Our goal in this book is to bring research on adolescent literacy and culturally responsive and sustaining pedagogies into conversation with research on trauma-sensitive instruction. We make practical suggestions about how English Language Arts teachers can support students through relevant instruction that builds resilience. This book is for the many teachers who are unsure how to invite students and their traumas into classroom instruction and embed these critical discussions and learning within their teaching practices and pedagogy. We hope to help all students, especially those affected by trauma, learn to "deal critically and creatively with reality and discover how to participate in the transformation of their world" (Shaull, 2000, p. 34). To begin, let us take a closer look at what trauma is.

WHAT IS TRAUMA?

The Substance Abuse and Mental Health Services Administration (SAMHSA), a federally funded agency that supports substance abuse and mental health programs across the United States, defines trauma as follows:

> Individual trauma results from an *event*, series of events, or set of circumstances that is *experienced* by an individual as physically or emotionally harmful or life-threatening and that has lasting adverse *effects* on the individual's functioning and mental, physical, social, emotional, or spiritual well-being. (SAMHSA, 2014, p. 7)

Thus, trauma consists of the three Es: events, experiences, and effects. These events are acute, chronic, or complex trauma. Acute trauma results from a single event, such as an automobile accident. Chronic trauma is ongoing, repeated exposure over an extended period of time, such as living in a war zone or an ongoing global pandemic. Finally, complex trauma deals with multiple traumatic events causing long-term impacts, such as profound neglect or abuse. According to the *Diagnostic and Statistical Manual of Mental Disorders* (DSM-5), a handbook used by health care professionals in the United States and much of the world as the authoritative guide to diagnosing mental disorders, trauma cannot exist without an event or series of events.

Experiences of Trauma

The second E in SAMSHA's definition, Experience, highlights that not all individuals will experience the same or similar event (or set of events) as traumatic. This means that one person may experience a situation as traumatic, while another may not. One's experiences of trauma are often influenced by an individual's developmental phase of life, an individual or group's cultural beliefs, and/or the availability of social supports, often called *protective factors* (Craig, 2017).

For instance, while isolated at home at the start of the pandemic, I (Rachelle) regularly walked my dog, Mocha Shake. While we were walking one day, a neighbor's dog brutally attacked Mocha Shake, and she succumbed to her wounds the next day. While the loss of a pet saddens most people, I was inconsolable. You see, Mocha was not only my fur baby but also my best friend. She was my father's pooch, and when he passed away, his only wish was that I take her with me. Mocha and I thus shared many memories, including the last connection with my father. Because of this most profound connection to Mocha—and because she was attacked—I experienced Mocha's death as deeply traumatic, whereas others may experience the loss of a pet with sadness but without categorizing the event as traumatic. We offer this story as an example of one essential aspect of trauma: There isn't a hierarchy to trauma or to someone else's experiences. One hardship is not more significant than another, nor can we judge the severity of others' traumas from the outside.

Instead, how one responds to trauma is often related to the number of risk factors one experiences and the number of protective factors to which one has access. Carlson and her colleagues (2016) explain that "factors that operate before trauma may directly or indirectly affect vulnerability to traumatic stress and risk for disorder, and later factors may exacerbate or ameliorate negative emotional responses to extreme stress" (p. 107). It is essential to know that as risk factors become more frequent and numerous, there tend to be fewer protective factors, causing a harmful imbalance. Risk and protective factors may occur at the individual level. For example, a genetic predisposition to anxiety might be a risk factor, whereas positive self-esteem and a strong sense of identity and selfhood can be protective factors.

However, risk and protective factors may also occur at the school level. For instance, institutional racism, the inability to connect and build relationships with peers, and bullying are risk factors at the school level. Nevertheless, we can help students build resilience by incorporating protective factors in our classrooms: having a consistent structure with clear expectations; building strong peer-to-peer and teacher-to-student relationships; supporting the development of prosocial skills, such as cooperation and empathy; and creating connectedness. These protective factors result in improved language and academic outcomes (Fisher et al., 2020; Holmes et al. 2018). We can create classrooms and school cultures that promote the development and growth of internal and external protective factors, such as good reasoning skills and civility (Henderson, 2013).

Benard's (1991) framework for building students' resilience highlights four main traits of resilient students: social competence, problem-solving skills, a sense of autonomy, and a sense of purpose with the belief in a bright future. In short, these traits are invaluable protective factors that can help students mitigate the adverse impacts of traumatic experiences. Across the traits, Benard identifies 19 observable outcomes that build students' resilience (see Table 1.1). These are not necessarily skills to be taught, as often presented in scripted SEL programs. Instead, they are evidence that students are building resilience.

These outcomes are, in our view, a solid answer to the question: What is resilience? For example, resilience while problem solving involves the ability to make plans, seek out help, and call upon creative and critical thinking to find solutions. Resilience as a social competency includes strong communication skills, a sense of humor, and empathy for others. These, in turn, assume

Table 1.1. Observable Outcomes That Build Student Resilience

Social Competence	Problem Solving
• Responsiveness • Cultural flexibility • Empathy • Caring • Communication skills • Sense of humor	• Planning • Help-seeking • Critical and creative thinking
Autonomy	**Sense of Purpose and Belief in a Bright Future**
• Sense of identity • Self-efficacy • Self-awareness • Task-mastery • Adaptive distancing from negative messages and conditions	• Goal direction • Educational aspirations • Optimism • Faith • Spiritual connectedness

that resilience is based on a sense of autonomy, which requires students to have a strong sense of their own identities, to believe in their self-efficacy, and—whenever possible—to distance themselves from negative situations and messages. All of these, in turn, relate to the fact that resilient people tend to have a strong sense of purpose and optimism about their futures.

Effects of Trauma

SAMHSA's (2014) final E, Effects, highlights that the effects of trauma may have an immediate or delayed onset and may be short or long term. For example, the collective and individual trauma of the global pandemic, which is a chronic event, will result in various experiences of that trauma. The pandemic may lead students to experience many potentially traumatic events. As of 2021, one in three people in the United States reported knowing someone who died of COVID-19. Others may experience food insecurity, increased exposure to domestic abuse, or loneliness, while some may have found online schooling preferable to in-person instruction. In addition, the onset of trauma may vary for individuals. As teachers, we are in a position to help. We can take a proactive stance to support our students both emotionally and intellectually.

TRAUMA IN SCHOOLS

Although we all probably like to think of schools as places where students arrive to be nurtured and supported through their experiences of trauma, research continues to highlight that schools are often places that marginalize—and sometimes traumatize or retraumatize—children. For example, in the United States, education news has consistently included high-profile mass shootings, such as those at Columbine, Newtown, Parkland, and Uvalde, as well as frequent gun violence between individuals. In total, between December 2012—the month of the massacre at Sandy Hook Elementary in Newtown—and the year 2019, children in the United States witnessed over 300 shootings—all of them at school (Noguera, 2019). Gun violence in schools is a source of collective trauma that impacts an entire community or population, with which our society must better reckon, and we offer it as just one example of how schools must attend to students' need for physical safety.

Yet, physical safety is not the only concern with which educators and students must grapple. Emotional safety is also paramount, but schools are too often places where students—and their cultures, backgrounds, and experiences—are devalued and demeaned. As educators, we are beginning to understand how structural, social, and political factors—such as systemic and institutional racism, grade retention and tracking, and inequitable educational opportunities—influence individual students' experiences of school (Dutro, 2019; Howard, 2017). Put more directly, schools are places where dominant narratives about who has value and potential in a society—usually white, cis-gendered, heteronormative, abled, English-speaking, middle-class men (Romero et al., 2018)—undervalue and marginalize students who do not fit into those boxes. Those with less power—those whose voices are marginalized—are often "forced to navigate the views of others in order to survive while seeing their own views minimized, othered, or outright ignored" (Mirra, 2018, p. 7).

Such silencing is problematic for all students and may lead to varying types of trauma, including racial, generational, and secondary trauma. Racial and generational trauma understands that trauma is "personal *and* shared," "part of the human condition *and* systemically targeted." It is "carried into schools *and* as inflicted by schools and systems of schooling" as well as "arising from oppressive systems of societies and institutions that create or exacerbate pain, loss, and struggle" (Dutro & Caasi, 2022, p. 360). Therefore, generational trauma passes on through families and communities (Dutro, 2019; Love, 2019) such as racism and systemic oppression. Secondary trauma occurs when someone learns of someone else's traumatic experience, such as reading graphic social media posts of the horrific situation people are enduring at an immigration facility, or listening to a parent, sibling, or friend describe discriminatory treatment in school. Reading these posts and witnessing other people's deplorable conditions can cause secondary trauma.

Thus, we want to highlight that although many educators are actively working to empower and uplift the voices of all students, schools have been among the many institutions in the United States that have disempowered and marginalized groups of students, especially students of color, students whose primary language is not English, students from low socioeconomic backgrounds, and LGTBQ+ students (e.g., Gutierrez et al., 2009). Of course, disempowerment and marginalization of members of specific demographics often originate from stereotypes. The experience of being stereotyped doesn't necessarily rise to the level of traumatization (though it certainly can), but we think it's important to highlight that stereotypes have a deleterious effect on learning. Fortunately, we also know that the risks of stereotype threat can be abated when educators carefully present academic tasks in ways that subvert stereotypes (Fisher et al., 2020).

HOW DOES TRAUMA INFLUENCE LEARNING?

Children and young adults may have difficulty coping with emotionally painful situations or experiences, impacting health, learning, behavior, and relationships (Cole et al., 2013; Craig, 2017; McLeod et al., 2012; Perry, 2014). Students experiencing trauma may have difficulty focusing, so they may struggle to understand the content or to process classroom instructions or expectations. They may also struggle with memory, especially recall of lessons and information learned. In addition, Perry (2014) stresses that students experiencing trauma may have a heightened focus on nonverbal cues, including the tone of another's voice or their facial expressions and posture. When a student makes a mistake or does not know how to process a difficult situation, they may blame others (Romero et al., 2018) or react in a flight/fight/freeze stance (Fisher et al., 2020; Hammond, 2015). They may not know how to self-regulate, which is the ability to monitor and manage emotions, thoughts, and behaviors. Also, many students experiencing trauma may frequently be absent, demonstrate behavioral issues, or drop out of school. All these factors challenge academic performance (Meyers, 2014; Rumsey & Milsom, 2019).

Unfortunately, when students display these behaviors, teachers may assume they are academically behind, have behavior issues, or both. This dynamic creates an unhealthy teacher–student relationship and can impede learning (O'Drobinak & Kelley, 2021, p. 36). Yet, we can support students' understanding of self-regulation and resilience by creating environments that harness their intrinsic motivations and desires. Osher and colleagues (2014) posited that "schools may function as a protective factor, creating a safe harbor, offering both challenge and a sense of mission, fostering positive relationships with adults and peers, developing competencies and a sense of efficacy, and providing students with access to social capital, mental health supports, and leadership opportunities" (p. 2). A positive teacher–student relationship that validates a student's experiences and explores problem-solving steps is similar to the therapeutic relationship between a therapist and his clients (Hammond, 2015).

HOW CAN SCHOOLS BECOME MORE SUPPORTIVE PLACES?

Fortunately, many schools do take trauma-informed or trauma-sensitive approaches to support students. These terms are often used interchangeably, and we will lean on a trauma-sensitive approach in this book. From SAMSHA's (2014) perspective, four assumptions underpin a trauma-informed approach to managing organizations. The four assumptions are that all people within organizations

(1) have a general understanding of trauma and its impact on people;
(2) recognize the signs and symptoms of trauma;
(3) provide training on evidence-based trauma practices; and
(4) learn ways to avoid re-traumatizing individuals. (pp. 9–10)

SAMSHA (2014) then lays out six key principles fundamental to a trauma-informed approach, as shown in Table 1.2.

SAMHSA provides resources, training, and evidence-based programs to support organizations in understanding the nature of trauma, which can better inform policy and practices at the organizational level. For instance, school counselors often use this lens to focus on leading professional learning on systemic and targeted interventions (Rumsey & Milsom, 2019). In short, trauma-informed approaches are about being aware of trauma to change policy. Teachers need these forms of awareness, and we will return to the six principles outlined above, describing how we can speak to them in the context of teaching English Language Arts throughout this book.

We also rely on research on trauma-sensitive schools to inform our work. The mission of research on trauma-sensitive schools is to address "trauma's impact on learning on a school-wide basis" (The Trauma and Learning Policy Initiative [TLPI], n.d.). Although the literature on trauma-sensitive schools emphasizes that educators are not expected to take on the role of therapist, it does insist that all school personnel have a responsibility not only to be aware of trauma—as trauma-informed approaches require—but also to participate in creating and sustaining the following six attributes of trauma-sensitive schools:

1. Leadership and staff share an understanding of trauma's impacts on learning and the need for a school-wide approach.
2. The school supports all students [to feel] safe physically, socially, emotionally, and academically.
3. The school addresses students' needs in holistic ways, taking into account their relationships, self-regulation, academic competence, and physical and emotional well-being.
4. The school explicitly connects students to the school community and provides multiple opportunities to practice newly developing skills.

5. The school embraces teamwork, and staff share responsibility for all students.
6. Leadership and staff anticipate and adapt to the ever-changing needs of students. (Cole et al., 2013, p. 18)

Although most teachers are not licensed or specifically trained to work with issues of trauma, English Language Arts teachers can still design and implement instruction that helps students see that we want to support them and that our subject matter is relevant to their real lived experiences—however painful. Such instruction opens lines of communication for our students, which can support resilience-building (Craig, 2017). The best teaching

Table 1.2. SAMSHA's Six Key Principles

Safety	Individuals have a right to feel "physically and psychologically safe; the physical setting is safe and interpersonal interactions promote a sense of safety" (p. 11).
Trustworthiness & Transparency	"[O]rganizational operations and decisions are conducted with transparency with the goal of building and maintaining trust" (p. 11).
Peer Support	"[P]eer support and mutual self-help are key vehicles for establishing safety and hope, building trust, enhancing collaboration, and utilizing their stories and lived experience to promote recovery and healing" (p. 11). Here, SAMSHA defines peers as others who have experienced trauma.
Collaboration & Mutuality	Guiding principles include the importance of "leveling power differences," "the sharing of power and decision making," and believing that "everyone has a role to play" (p. 11).
Empowerment & Choice	Trauma-informed organizations should recognize and build upon "individuals' strengths and experiences," believe in the ability to heal and recover from trauma, and understand that, historically, power differentials diminish "voice and choice," which can lead to "coercive treatment," and a need for the "cultivation of self-advocacy skills" (p. 11).
Cultural, Historical, & Gender Issues	A trauma-informed organization also understands the "healing value of traditional cultural connections; incorporates policies, protocols, and processes that are responsive to the racial, ethnic, and cultural needs of individuals served; and recognizes and addresses historical trauma" (p. 11).

"encourages students to develop the capacity to name the world for themselves, to identify the obstacles to their full humanity, and to have the courage to act upon whatever the unknown demands" (Ayers & Ayers, 2014, p. 13). It also engages and challenges students throughout their learning (Hattie, 2012) by connecting students' lived experiences with our curricula. This book is thus devoted to laying out why ELA teachers might want to take up trauma-sensitive instructional approaches and show that its benefits far outweigh the risks for students, society, and you, the teacher.

For more information on ACEs, we recommend visiting the Centers for Disease Control and Prevention webpage devoted to ACEs (cdc.gov/violenceprevention/aces/index.html). It provides you with information, videos, resources, and additional links for preventing ACEs, Risk and Protective Factors, Fast Facts, research and case studies, and others. The Philadelphia ACEs Project website (philadelphiaaces.org) provides additional information related to its ACEs survey, community-level stressors, and adult health issues. Another website, ACEs Too High, is a news site that reports on research about positive and adverse childhood experiences, including developments in epidemiology, neurobiology, and the biomedical and epigenetic consequences of toxic stress, according to their website (acestoohigh.com). Additionally, we recommend the following resources to learn more about ACEs and trauma-sensitive schools: the 10-item Adverse Childhood Experience (ACE) Questionnaire about experiences before age 18 (Felitti et al., 1998; Fisher et al., 2020); the Addressing Race and Trauma in the Classroom Resource (nctsn.org/sites/default/files/resources/addressing_race_and_trauma_in_the_classroom_educators.pdf); and the Trauma-Sensitive School Checklist (learningforjustice.org/sites/default/files/general/trauma%20sensitive%20school%20checklist%20(1).pdf).

THE PURPOSE OF THIS BOOK

This book stems from a book Rachelle co-authored with Drs. Douglas Fisher and Nancy Frey, entitled *Teaching Hope and Resilience for Students Experiencing Trauma: Creating Safe and Nurturing Classrooms for Learning*. In that book, Rachelle and her colleagues provided an extensive background on trauma, its relationship to teaching and learning, the power of relationships, and how SEL can be embedded within a curriculum. In addition, the book devoted a chapter to describing how teachers can use literacies to maximize learning and teach for empowerment. We know that literacy is not just a skill for our students to possess but also a tool to help them stand up for themselves and their needs (Muhammad, 2020).

The book you have in your hands builds upon that work, utilizing the authors' knowledge and background in trauma-sensitive instruction, adolescent literacy, and culturally responsive and sustaining pedagogies to provide practical ways that English Language Arts teachers, in particular, can support students experiencing trauma while they are helping students to reach the standards in the English Language Arts. Specifically, our work lies within a critical literacy framework (Bishop, 2014; Vasquez et al., 2019), touching upon SEL (Fisher et al., 2020; Frey et al., 2019; Ippolito & Savitz, 2022) to support you—the reader—to create instruction that is more equitable, more intellectually rigorous, and more open and caring for students experiencing trauma. In short, our book provides a rationale and model for how teachers can respond to and incorporate trauma issues to support students' academic growth in literacy and, more specifically, in the English Language Arts.

Throughout this book, we will advocate for building relationships with students in and through shared engagement with content. We will highlight ways to position students as participants in the discourse of English Language Arts to show students that their experiences of topics germane to ELA are important to the class's learning. We will continue to highlight that, in trauma-sensitive literacy instruction, students must have repeated opportunities to share aspects of who they are and to make connections between those aspects of themselves and the curricula. We will describe how doing so is intellectually and emotionally invaluable work for students, and we will offer several strategies teachers can use to do this in ELA.

We will also provide guidance and practical solutions through literacy tools and ideas for teachers to navigate student trauma in a way that empowers students and teachers. We will explain how theory supports these practices and provide examples so that teachers can understand how to embed this necessary work within their classrooms. We will connect with the typical ELA curriculum and unit themes and provide additional nontraditional routes, such as using young adult literature and critical inquiry.

It is important to note that various vignettes and examples come from our classroom conversations with students, teachers we work with, and current research. None of the chapters intends to be taken as gospel or used wholesale. The examples we provide are not intended to be replicated exactly as we present them. Instead, we hope you will consider your students' and your community's specific interests, strengths, and concerns to build on what we suggest here. In addition, we will provide helpful resources. We include actual teacher names with their permission and use pseudonyms for students and others who prefer to remain anonymous.

As educators, we feel it is vital to be aware of all types of traumatic experiences and to understand that 38% of students in the United States are impacted daily and yearly (Robert Wood Johnson Foundation, 2017). It is also crucial to recognize that our practices, school policies, and institutional cultures can traumatize students at school (Gorski, 2020).

WHO ARE WE AND WHY ARE WE WRITING THIS BOOK?

As authors, we want to share who we are and why we feel we are the "right" people to write this book. Before becoming scholars and teacher educators, we were both teachers and worked in K–12 classrooms for 18 years combined. Although neither of us is a licensed mental health professional, school counselor, or school psychologist, we have witnessed, observed, and worked with students deeply influenced by various traumas and have, of course, experienced many traumatic situations.

As educators, we seek to understand how trauma impacts students' lives and learning. These experiences have spurred us to better understand trauma in classrooms and how to support equitable teaching in secondary literacy. Because we have also both used, taught, and studied SEL, trauma-sensitive practices, culturally responsive and sustaining pedagogies, and various approaches to incorporating critical literacy in instruction, we see unique connections that we will share with teachers. Since we both are researchers in secondary literacy instruction, we will also point out along the way how trauma-sensitive instruction can support not only kids experiencing trauma—which is good for students and the SEL aspects of your classroom—but also how such an approach can help your students' growth as stronger listeners, speakers, readers, writers, and viewers of increasingly complex text.

We also want to be clear about our positionality. As white, cisgender, and heterosexual educators, we understand that we lack the expertise related to all of the background and nuance surrounding potential cultural stigma associated with specific traumatic experiences. We also recognize that many traumatic experiences arise because of inequities faced within and outside of the classroom (DiAngelo, 2018; Love, 2019).

Instead, what we bring is a commitment to ensuring that students can bring who they are and what they know into classrooms so that they—and their peers—can more deeply make sense of the English Language Arts and see its questions and concerns as relevant to their own lives and the lives of those they love. We have learned much about how we can do this in ways that support students experiencing trauma, and we'd like to share it with you.

care for students can positively or negatively impact students' school experiences and that "true empathy lies in carefully listening to others to hear their thoughts and feelings" (p. 771). Luckily, there are many qualities that a caring teacher may possess, with the main emphasis on knowing and valuing every student. This means that we need to take a holistic view of students, seeking to understand not only their academic needs but also their personal needs related to their hardships and challenges (Zacarian & Soto, 2020). Hertel and Johnson (2013) add that making students feel valued, respected, and safe means that teachers must do the following:

1. Always empower and never disempower.
2. Provide unconditional positive regard.
3. Maintain high expectations.
4. Check assumptions, observe, and question.
5. Be a relationship coach.
6. Provide opportunities for meaningful participation. (pp. 31–32)

If you are interested in thinking through your relationships with students, you may want to try the Student–Teacher Relationship Scale, which "measures a teacher's perception of conflict, closeness, and dependency with a specific child" (Pianta, 1992, n.p.). Or you may use Elena Aguilar's (2020) free online teacher-to-student interaction tracking tool found on her website (brightmorningteam.com/coaching-for-equity-tools), first introduced in her 2013 book, *The Art of Coaching: Effective Strategies for School Transformation.*

Fortunately, research has found that most teachers enter the profession with a desire to be a caring teacher; in interviews, beginning teachers often avow that they want to "be nice to their students, to demonstrate understanding and sympathy, and to ensure that students [feel] safe in school" (Kennedy, 1998, p. 18). You are probably reading this book because you agree. Yet, we must also be aware that when we followed those same teachers into classrooms, many beginning teachers wanted compliance from students. They wanted to be recognized as the authority in the classroom, and they "wanted to be at least benevolent in their exercise of authority" (p. 20). We should be careful here because it's easy for all of us to confuse the benevolent exercise of authority with caring, but they are not the same thing. In fact, Rachelle has a great story about this from her first year of teaching:

I (Rachelle) remember going home each night, thinking about how disrespectful my students were. I decided to discuss this with them the following day. After receiving nothing but blank stares and a few grumbles, one young man bravely stated, "We don't respect teachers because teachers haven't earned respect." Wow! This brief moment was a huge wake-up call for me. I remember being told in my teacher education program that classroom management was the key. If I were strict and structured, my students would "cooperate." The goal was for them to align with what I wanted.

I thought of myself as the expert sharing knowledge, and they would be passive listeners waiting to be told what to know. In my first year, I had assumed that students would go by the old adage "respect your elders." I did not consider how I had to prove myself as a caring adult who believed all my students could succeed. Thus, I had not gained my students' respect or trust. That simple lesson was pivotal in my early years of teaching and pushed my rethinking teaching and instruction. I want to be a guide on the side, not the sage on the stage.

In Rachelle's story, we can see how insightful students can be: They knew, somewhere deep down, that they were not respected; they were to comply, and compliance is not part of the ethic of caring about, which Nel Noddings (2012; 2013) wrote. Expecting compliance will also fail to build critical thinkers in an English Language Arts class. Thus, we must carefully differentiate caring from compliance when teaching and working with students. This is especially vital for students who have experienced trauma, as trauma already puts into place a "power differential where one entity (whether an individual, an event, or a force of nature) has power over another" (SAMHSA, 2014, p. 8). If a student feels that their teacher does not care about them, or expects compliance without question, then that power differential continues to tip away from the student.

We bring up this discussion of care and compliance to highlight an important idea: Just because we are told that we need to care for our students doesn't mean that we always have clear ideas about how to do that effectively, particularly for our students who have experienced or are experiencing trauma. As Nieto and Bode (2018) remind us, "care is not a single-dimensional activity or concept" (p. 216). Instead, it's a mindset that can be made manifest through a wide variety of action-oriented teaching practices. These practices might involve making minor changes to our teaching, such as ensuring that we correctly pronounce each of our students' names, or through practices that are much, much bigger, such as designing entire academic units in ways that allow students to leverage and build on what they have learned both in and out of school.

Based on our synthesis of a wide breadth of research, which we briefly describe in the next section, we present a framework for specifying what it means to care for our students, particularly when they are experiencing or have experienced trauma. Before we explain the five aspects of this framework, however, we would like to say a few words about the research upon which we drew in writing this book.

THE RESEARCH BASE FOR THIS BOOK

As is true of all books, this is not the final word, nor are we the ultimate experts on trauma-sensitive literacy instruction. Instead, this is our best attempt to make sense of research in a complicated and invaluable area: how to support students experiencing trauma in ELA classes. To do so, we built on socio-emotional learning (SEL) research, as might be expected for a book on trauma-sensitive literacy instruction. After all, a focus on SEL is currently all the rage in educational circles, and several fine books have recently published on the subject, including those listed in the following textbox.

However, too often, fads in education—such as the current focus on socio-emotional learning (SEL)—start in a good-hearted place. In this case, the focus on SEL comes from educators' genuine concern with how students' SEL influences their academic outcomes and life experiences. However, this good-heartedness runs the risk of becoming, in practice, a set of stand-alone practices or programs that are grafted inadequately onto an already over-full curriculum or wedged into a "homeroom" class that rarely meets.

We hope to help educators avoid this eventuality. Thus, we draw upon work on SEL because SEL touches on essential principles related to trauma. However, we wrote this book because we know that teachers have access to instructional strategies that are both trauma-sensitive and content-specific.

Recommended Books for Further Learning on SEL

All Learning Is Social and Emotional: Helping Students Develop Essential Skills for the Classroom and Beyond by Nancy Frey, Douglas Fisher, and Dominique Smith, published by Association for Supervision and Curriculum Development.

Navigating SEL from the Inside Out: Looking Inside and Across 33 Leading SEL Programs. A Practical Resource for Schools and OST Providers by Stephanie Jones, Katharine Brush, Rebecca Bailey, Gretchen Brion-Meisels, Joseph McIntyre, Jennifer Kahn, Bryan Nelson, and Laura Stickle, published by the Harvard Graduate School of Education and the Wallace Foundation.

Safe and Sound: An Educational Leader's Guide to Evidence-Based Social and Emotional Learning (SEL) Programs written and published by the Collaborative for Academic, Social, and Emotional Learning (CASEL).

Teaching Hope and Resilience for Students Experiencing Trauma: Creating Safe and Nurturing Classrooms for Learning by Douglas Fisher, Nancy Frey, and Rachelle Savitz, published by Teachers College Press.

The Practice Base for How We Learn: Supporting Students' Social, Emotional, and Academic Development by Sheldon Berman, Sydney Chaffee, and Julia Sarmiento, published by the Aspen Institute, National Commission on Social, Emotional, and Academic Development.

By synthesizing research in SEL and trauma with work in adolescent literacy, disciplinary literacy, and culturally responsive-sustaining instruction, we can speak directly to the concerns and responsibilities of ELA teachers. We believe this synthesis is the main contribution of this work, and we want to clarify why we have chosen to extend work on socio-emotional learning and trauma-sensitive instruction in these ways.

We drew on research in adolescent literacy because it gives us insight into how students' developmental age—middle and high school is the focus of this book—influence literacy development and instruction. We drew on research in disciplinary literacy because this research helps to understand literacy expectations specific to English Language Arts. Our decision to rely on research in culturally responsive and sustaining pedagogies, which focuses specifically on empowering disempowered students, primarily because of racism, classism, and language differences (Alim & Paris, 2017; Ladson-Billings, 1995), may seem less obvious.

Some may assume that we see trauma-sensitive literacy instruction merging with the tenets of culturally responsive and sustaining pedagogies and equity because students of color and students who grow up in poverty are more likely to experience trauma. Although this is true, we do not want the implication to be that students of color and students growing up in poverty do not experience rich lives full of joy (they do) or that middle- and upper-class white students do not experience trauma (they do). Instead, we have chosen to think about trauma-sensitive literacy instruction through the lens of culturally responsive and sustaining pedagogies because a resounding finding about students experiencing trauma—regardless of their race, socioeconomic status, and other demographic characteristics—is that they feel that their experience is shameful, which often leads them to feel alone and marginalized at school (SAMHSA, 2014). Thus, we draw on research on culturally responsive and sustaining pedagogies because this research is foundationally concerned with ensuring that students do not feel marginalized (e.g., Ladson-Billings, 1995; Paris & Alim, 2017).

FIVE PILLARS OF TRAUMA-SENSITIVE LITERACY INSTRUCTION: A FRAMEWORK

Based on these various bodies of research, we have identified five crucial skill sets teachers can use to create classrooms where students are supported to build resilience while developing literacies in English Language Arts. Trauma-sensitive literacy teachers

- investigate our own biases;
- share our vulnerability;
- promote choice;

- foster students' academic competence by designing instruction that builds on who students are and what they already know; and
- foster peer–peer relationships that honor multiple perspectives

As you will see, these pillars are ultimately inseparable and interdependent, but we describe them individually for clarity.

Pillar I: Investigate Our Own Implicit Biases

Being trustworthy and caring involves a willingness to take a sometimes soul-ripping journey into the heart of our implicit biases. This is important because students are often aware of our racial, cultural, socioeconomic, academic, or personality-based biases, even if we are not. For example, Britnie's sister Kailey was, for many years, a teacher in a rural school on one of South Carolina's Sea Islands, where the students were predominantly Black, and generational poverty could be traced precisely to the time of slavery. Britnie and Kailey's parents would be visiting from Colorado in the coming days, and they had asked if they could have lunch with Kailey at school. If they arrived a few minutes early, they hoped they could see a few minutes of her teaching and perhaps even meet her students. Kailey asked her students if that would be all right:

> "Yeah, right," one boy called out from the back: "Your parents don't want to meet us. If they saw me on the street, they'd cross it. Your mom would grab your dad's arm, and say, 'Oh, Phil. They're so close to me.'"

This student's comment was funny, incisive, poignant, and sad, revealing how he experienced a deep racial rift between white families like ours and Black families like his. We include this story to highlight that students are aware of the implicit biases of individual teachers and larger cultural groups and that these are continuously operating in classrooms. My sister's student decided to surface his discomfort with those potential biases, but more often, implicit biases remain just that: implicit. Indeed, this secretiveness allows such bias to remain and become incredibly corrosive (Milner, 2021).

Research highlights that teachers' implicit biases often take the form of deficit mindsets toward students, which—at base—tend to assume that students are, for any number of reasons, somehow broken or unable to learn (Milner, 2021; Nieto & Bode, 2018). This is often particularly true for students who are experiencing or have experienced trauma. In Raylea's case, for instance, many school-based personnel understood Raylea chiefly in terms of what she could not or did not do: She did not do her homework, she could not be quiet, she did not consistently come to school, and the list went on. As Spencer and colleagues' research (1999) on stereotype threat points out, we should be cautious about framing our students in these ways, as stereotypes can influence reality. First, constantly interpreting students in the negative works against efforts to help students build resilience and flies in the face of research on teaching those who have experienced trauma. These studies often highlight that a teacher's main role is to position students, always, as agentive and capable. As Bandura's (1977) seminal research on self-efficacy highlighted long ago, just like adults, students learn best when they have high self-efficacy. Students must feel they can achieve success in tackling more challenging situations.

Not only are such deficit mindsets harmful to students, they can also negatively affect the intellectual quality of our instruction. Recent research on mathematics education makes this point clear: In an 8-year study funded by the National Science Foundation, researchers (including Britnie) followed hundreds of teachers (Cobb et al., 2018). These teachers took tests intended to measure how much they understood about transforming content-specific concepts in ways that would be conceptually clear to students (Boston & Wilhelm, 2017). They were also interviewed about how much they understood highly effective, conceptually rich instruction (Munter, 2014) and how much they believed in students' academic capabilities (Jackson et al., 2018). Then, researchers watched videos of teachers teaching. Take a guess: Which of these factors—specialized forms of content-knowledge that allow teachers to make concepts available to students; teachers' ability to describe exactly what highly effective instruction looks like; or teachers' belief in students' capabilities—most influenced the quality of their instruction? You got it: Teachers' belief in students' capabilities was the essential and irreplaceable difference between those who truly served students and those who didn't. Teachers might have a deep understanding of conceptually rich instruction or astounding content knowledge, but if they do not believe in their student's academic capabilities, their instruction won't reflect the strength of their content knowledge or pedagogical expertise. The truth is that when we make assumptions or view students through a negative lens, we are part of why they may not be successful (Park et al., 2018).

Here's an example of one common way our implicit biases operate: Most of us are familiar with the well-worn practice of asking students about their summer vacations in the early days of school. Writing assignments about summer vacations have enshrined in popular culture, and the practice continues—for many of us—precisely because we care about our students and want to know about their lives. Or, as you are reading this, perhaps you think that the summer vacation assignment is more typical of elementary school; as a secondary teacher, you prefer to ask students questions about their families and lives. Again, this practice often comes from a good place. However, it is essential to remember that asking students to recount personal details in front of the class is not always an unqualified good. Even seemingly innocuous questions about families or where students spent their summer vacation can weaken an already frail sense of belonging, trigger students, or—in some cases—cause retraumatization. The reason is that these questions are based on multiple assumptions about our students, their home lives, and the resources they have access to. Questions about families and summer vacations assume that students know their families and that the relationships are positive—or at least neutral—enough to be viable subjects for casual, public conversation. Questions about summer vacations imply that all students have money and the ability to travel over summer break. Both assume that students feel comfortable sharing this information with others. So, Marie, a girl who was kicked out of her house over the summer, may choose to avoid this assignment—and also to avoid you and her peers. Or, let's consider Marko, who had to work the entire summer to help support his family, taking any free time to babysit his two younger siblings.

Jacqueline Woodson characterizes the problem well in her poem, published as a children's book, called *The Day You Begin* (2018). In it, a young girl recounts how her summer vacation was spent reading books with her little sister, and she longs for the vacations to Long Island and South Carolina that her peers describe. When asked to narrate her summer vacation, the girl describes her "own voice, once huge, now smaller" because the experience is one of isolation. Here, Woodson (2018) helps us to see how a sense of belonging, so often a fragile thing, can be damaged by seemingly innocuous, well-meaning questions. This is not to say that questions about summer vacation are necessarily traumatizing—however, it is to say that students must feel they belong—personally, academically, socially, and culturally—in classrooms, and those who have or are experiencing trauma need this sense of belonging even more.

The most immediate question on your mind might simply be: How can I get to know students when I don't know what they've been through, and—apparently—I can't ask them simple questions because those might, unwittingly, be an example of my own implicit bias or even retraumatizing? Don't worry: It's not as cruel a catch-22 as that. We can and should continue to ask authentic questions of our students, not just at the beginning of the year but daily. Yet, we must first be more reflective about it. One alternative is for teachers to invite students to share one thing about them that they want teachers to know about their lives and/or families. Trauma-sensitive literacy instruction asks that we hand students much more power—the power to choose what they share with others, the power to make decisions about their self-presentation, and even the power to decide which aspects of their lives they will draw upon to access academic ideas. The summer vacation exercise is a prime example of instructional decision-making that, though often rooted in a desire to get to know students, is not empowering in the ways many students need.

Another option is to start by asking students about their favorite book, character, genre, plot, and so on. In this case, it's important to follow up by telling students that they can also share their favorite TV show, movie, blog, or videogame. Why? Again, we want to position students—all students—in ways that empower them. Calling students out for not having the resources to travel or not having a favorite book is—by definition—not an empowering practice, and it won't engender a sense of trust between you and your students. Of course, TV shows, blogs, and video games are also important to literacy, and we say more about that later in the book.

Thus, implicit biases are powerful aspects of classroom practice, so we must consistently check our own. For white educators interested in exploring their own implicit biases, we refer you to the work of Janet Helms (1990) and her six-status model that is divided into two meta-processes: abandonment of racism and defining a nonracist white identity. Or the work of Sue and Sue (2008), whose five-phase white racial identity development model views the process are more fluid and nonlinear. Additional scholarly recommendations include Ali Michael, Richard Milner, Christine Sleeter, Cheryl Matias, Bettina Love, James Jupp, among many others exploring white racial identity. Another place to start is by brainstorming your way through your development as a cultural being: What, in your upbringing, was assumed to be true and right? What was valued? What was not valued? What examples of unearned advantage influenced your development as a person? What about examples of unearned disadvantages? Questions like these help us better recognize our implicit biases' origins. For an excellent book on this subject, see H. R. Milner's *Start Where You Are, But Don't Stay There* (2021).

Of course, as we learn about our biases and assumptions, we are also teaching. There isn't a point when we become fully woke, reach Nirvana, and are finally ready to teach students who have experienced trauma. Instead, as teachers, we must teach all students—even those most vulnerable—while we remain imperfect mortals. And that means that our challenge remains to create authentic relationships that promote safety and resilience.

Pillar II: Providing Academic Choices

To support a culture of care in the classroom, we must step away from a culture of control in the classroom (Rios, 2017). One way to promote more student control is by offering choice. We can give students choices by providing opportunities to choose topics for research-based inquiry, what strategies they will use, which text(s) or genres of text they will read, whether they will work in small groups or with partners, and many other options.

You may have noticed that both of our alternative suggestions for common getting-to-know-you questions (e.g., the dreaded summer vacation question) empower students by giving them choices. In trauma-sensitive literacy teaching, this focus on choices extends throughout the academic curricula. Specifically, we can provide additional options to students by linking curricula to students' interests and life experiences (Allington, 2015), which encourages students to become personally involved in and accountable for their education. Who doesn't feel valued and cared for when learning connects to our beliefs, values, and interests?

Rachel Bolte, an English Language Arts teacher who has worked with Rachelle, shared the following about *why* she consistently modifies her lessons and offers students choices:

> I believe there is a need to intentionally choose/curate texts so that students feel represented and seen throughout the class and learn new perspectives. In my district, there is an intentional push to use culturally responsive texts that reflect our student population and give students insight into other perspectives. Currently, my student population is over 95% Latino. This means that when we focus on change-makers in society, we talk about the African American leaders of the Civil Rights Movement and Hispanic and Latinx leaders, Muslim leaders, female leaders, and others.
>
> And we must focus on the power and not only the oppression. For example, in years past, we had a unit focused on the oppression and atrocities against communities of color, specifically during the Jim Crow era. We, the teachers, revised our curriculum when we realized there was a sole focus on the atrocities and not enough on the individuals who fought back. This year, the unit focused on those fighting oppression—MLK, Malcolm X, Bryan Stevenson, and others. While we provided anchor texts for these change-makers, students were also encouraged to explore others who inspired them, leading to even more texts to share with the class. Students choose people and groups who stand out to them. For instance, many students chose activists who stood for something that reflected their identities, such as LGBTQIA+ activists, immigration activists, feminists, and others.

As Rachel reminds us, if we want our students to engage in learning, then we, as educators, also must reflect on how we are setting up students to do so.

Importantly, providing choice is not just important for helping empower students who have experienced trauma. The research on improving students' abilities as readers and writers is also clear about the value of offering choice because choice can be motivating. For example, when it comes to reading, we know that "students read more, understand more, and are more likely to continue reading when they have the opportunity to choose what they read" (Allington & Gabriel, 2012, p. 10). Providing choice in reading options may mean that the whole class reads one short story, and then students pick from an array of other short stories, poems, or informational texts that deal with the same essential question or a related concept under study (Smagorinsky, 2019). Alternatively, providing choice may mean incorporating literature circles instead of a whole-class novel. We will discuss these elements more in Chapter 3, but it is important to note here that, as educators, we have many ways to offer choice, which makes our students feel we consider their needs.

Pillar III: Sharing Vulnerabilities With Students

To build trust with students, we must share pieces of ourselves before we ask students to share pieces of themselves. As Rachelle's student in her first year of teaching put it, we must earn our students' respect, and we must also earn their trust. By sharing vulnerability, teachers model for students what it means to be vulnerable, and we open the door to what Dutro (2013) has called "reciprocal testimony," in which students and teachers reciprocally share their lives and—yes—sometimes even their shared or individual experiences of trauma. By sharing our vulnerabilities and struggles, we are also sharing that we are not perfect at everything we do and that everything isn't always perfect in our lives.

The concept of reciprocal testimony, which we will discuss in greater depth in Chapter 4, reminds me (Britnie) of an older, white male teacher with whom I once taught. Although I did not know him well, I did know that, among students, he was rumored to be the "racist" teacher. Let's call him Mr. Fields. At a faculty meeting once, someone asked Mr. Fields why he still taught and drove over an hour and a half—each way—to be with this group of students. He said that he loved his students, that he had grown up in extreme poverty and without a positive male role model in his life, and that he hoped to be that role model for his students. What might have happened had Mr. Fields shared these aspects of his upbringing with his students? Would such an admission have opened space for students to share their feelings of discomfort and distrust in his class? Would that have helped them all to open up a pathway toward common ground and, perhaps, even some shared empathy in Mr. Fields's racially charged classroom? I do not want to pretend that any of those conversations would have been easy. Nor should students, who are—by definition—at a power disadvantage when compared to teachers in schools, be responsible for explaining their experiences of racism to Mr. Fields. I suggest that, as teachers, we are responsible for being vulnerable first and allowing students to come through that door if they choose to do so (Dutro, 2019). Thus, one key to building trustworthiness and a classroom of care is beginning the process of being vulnerable with students.

D. Phelps, a teacher who works with Rachelle, describes how sharing vulnerability influences teaching in the ELA classroom:

> "Excavation leads to emancipation"; these are the words that have gradually become my mantra during my time in the classroom and in

my personal life. Sharing vulnerability and being open breaks barriers and emphasizes the importance of the power of being loved. Being open shows that educators are intentional in providing a brave space for students to come openly with their trauma, pain, and grief and freely be able to express themselves unapologetically.

We as educators must always recognize that there is so much more to our students than what we see. We must be intentional about getting to know our students and understanding their environmental layers. Put the curriculum aside and spend time fostering a true classroom community where we get to know the intimate details of our students' lives and how they function. This can include creative writing prompts, social-emotional learning, or hip-hop pedagogy to tie their musical tastes to the curriculum. Tie in their interests and be sure to find creative ways for them to amplify their unique voices.

When we share our emotions, we foster meaningful discussions applicable to their daily lives. We challenge students to think critically and outside the box. Students are encouraged to tackle emotions such as depression, grief, perfectionism, and even abandonment with various discussion forms because each person comes with a unique understanding of life, love, freedom, and emotions. Emotions equal freedom because you can't control when a certain emotion washes over you or rises within you. If schools are built on deep relationships, and consent is embedded in the relationship-building framework, we all learn how to be self-aware, recognize how others want to engage with us, and face our potential demons. We must prioritize freedom of expression through opportunities connecting the home and school settings. With vulnerability and this type of openness comes authenticity. Therefore, we as educators must be open and honest about our trauma, struggles, and grief to invite students to share more about themselves.

Pillar IV: Building From Who Students Are and What They Already Know

As a field, the learning sciences have known since Piaget (1971) that human learning builds from what we already know (Bransford et al., 2000; Bruner, 1977)). This is a significant idea that we will develop throughout the book, but we highlight that trauma-sensitive literacy instruction—indeed, all instruction—must proceed from what students know, not simply because Piaget said so, but because doing so can help students build resilience.

Indeed, evidence continues to build that educators must design instruction so that students' personal and cultural histories occupy important places within classroom academic discourse (Goldman et al., 2016; Muhammad, 2020). Researchers interested in culturally responsive and sustaining pedagogies (e.g., Ladson-Billings, 1995; Paris, 2012) have continually highlighted that teachers must substantively incorporate into curricula the ways of knowing and being that characterize students, their families, and communities, which Moll and his colleagues (1992) have called "funds of knowledge." The idea is that teachers can—and should—draw upon students' cultural experiences in daily instruction and embrace students' native languages and families as assets to help students draw on both dominant academic practices and their cultural ways of being and knowing to make sense of the world and find success within it (Gay, 2018; Nieto & Bode, 2018).

Jason DeHart, an English Language Arts teacher, describes for us how he brings students' lives into his classroom:

> Belonging is a human need I feel myself, and I know my students feel it. I vividly recall meetings mid-day in which I had to review test score data, including graphs with bright "good to go" greens and blaring "teach them better" reds. My students are more than graphs and test scores; focusing on what makes us human is part of why I am a literacy advocate and English teacher.
>
> Part of how I build a sense of belonging is by getting to know my students first and foremost, which probably sounds trite but is also true. I share family photos, stories about myself, and details about my interests. I invite my students to share about *themselves*, as they are comfortable in short writings and discussions. We discuss culture and life and, as much as possible, move beyond the assumptions that can be made about each other. When I have a student expressing a limited view of someone else, we return to the sense of kindness discussed in our first few class periods. In this way, I want my classroom to be a space that is safe and welcoming.
>
> Recently, we read a memoir in class that was part of our curriculum. I supplemented this with a section of "For Every One" by Jason Reynolds, in which he talks about his dreams and experiences. Following this reading/listening, I invited the students to share four events about their lives in a multimodal memoir. They could use images, drawings, quotes, English, Spanish, and more. Activities like this are a way to learn about my students and respond in writing/creating. Using quotes, song lyrics, and images is an additional invitation for students who aren't comfortable with writing. We can compose across languages for students who are more comfortable writing in another language. Comfort applies to the content area and the community we have in the classroom.
>
> While I recognize that we live in an age of test scores and labels, I don't deny my students quality experiences with rich and challenging texts

> based on scores or reading levels. I might support them more with some readings, but I try to remember that I have the power to speak into a student's life while recognizing that I cannot tell their future. I try to share invitations and opportunities with my students to read more and see literacy as something real that's not just about a class. We dabble in authors from long ago and read works that are on social media. We reach a range of texts so that students can see that authors speak from various lived experiences, including those who are not white and those who identify as men. All of my students belong, and I want them to receive that message very clearly—with kindness and respect that begins with me.

In other words, students must be shown, in substantive ways, that what they know and have experienced is valid, relevant, and essential to make sense of complex academic ideas (Ladson-Billings, 1995; Lee, 2007; Paris & Alim, 2012). Students need to see their own experiences in academic work if they are to learn and if they are to build positive identities as contributors to academic discourse. We are here to say that trauma is a part of most students' experience, so it is a part of what students know and from which they can learn. Including students' lives, experiences, and cultural practices in the official academic curriculum can help students feel respected and essential to the learning process (Gay, 2013). In other words, students develop cultural competence, and it is a process that supports teachers and students to move beyond deficit perspectives on students and communities so that teachers and students begin to see cultural differences as assets (Gay, 2013; Zacarian & Soto, 2020). We suggest that students who have or are experiencing trauma need opportunities to build their senses of self-efficacy and competence in the classroom and beyond.

Often, teachers interpret the need to build curricula from students' personal and cultural knowledge bases to mean that they should help students make connections to what they know and care about. That's true, but it overlooks the profound ways students' identities and cultural ways of being are woven through the curricula. We'll explain using Britnie's favorite example: the Kim Kardashian Syndrome. While I was teaching new teachers about the need to build curricula from students' personal and cultural histories, one new teacher raised her hand: "But I've tried that. I'm teaching about the Armenian Genocide, and the only thing kids know about Armenia is that Kim Kardashian is from there, so we talked for, like, 2 minutes about Kim Kardashian, and then that's it. Thirty seconds later, we've stopped talking about Kim Kardashian, they aren't interested anymore, and they are no closer to understanding anything about the Armenian Genocide!"

Like the teacher mentioned above, I'm sure you want something much deeper and more conceptually robust than this drive-by reference to a pop culture figure. In Britnie's teacher education courses, she's taken to calling this the Kim Kardashian Syndrome. It's relatively easy for our instruction to come down with this. Fortunately, Carol D. Lee, whose work has long focused on equitable teaching in English Language Arts, has an answer. Lee's (2007) work on cultural modeling still stands as one of the best theorized and well-developed examples of building from what students know in intellectually substantive ways. In her view, what's missing when our instruction comes down to the Kim Kardashian Syndrome is that excellent instruction needs to support students to have "well-developed identities as competent academic learners" (Lee, 2007, p. 29). She highlights that repeated failure—or even a history of mediocre performance—can hinder students' ability to build a sense of academic competence, as can "subject matter learning goals that are difficult to connect to their lived experiences or hopes for the future" (p. 29).

To help students rise above past failings or mediocrity, as well as students' oft-reported feeling that what they are learning is not relevant to their lives, Lee begins by connecting subject matter learning goals in deeply substantive ways to her students' cultural practices. She uses signifying, or "playing the dozens," to help students understand the metaphor. You've heard of "your mama" jokes, right? As in, "Your mama so old her social security number is one"? In academic circles, this is called signifying. What Lee (2007) brilliantly points out is that signifying embodies much of the academic thinking that English Language Arts values: Like reading the Bard himself, making sense of "Your Mama" jokes depends on an understanding of metaphor and inferential thinking.

In her research, Lee (2007) helped students to make this connection, and her findings were statistically significant: Students' sensemaking about key concepts in English Language Arts improved when students were supported to see the relationship between metaphors in signifying, for instance, and in poetry and fiction. In other words, Lee (2007) argued that students use the same reasoning skills to interpret "Yo mama so skinny she can do the hula hoop in a Cheerio" (Lee, 2007, p. 13) as they do to interpret "Four of his five wits went halting off, and now is the whole man governed with one . . ." (Shakespeare, *A Midsummer Night's Dream*, 1:1). Cool, right? This is much deeper and more substantive than mentioning Kim Kardashian. Drive-by references to pop culture figures don't surface the reasoning that students already know how to do, and they don't help students to see how those ways of reasoning are similar to the reasoning they will need to do in ELA. In short, they don't position students as academically valued and valuable.

We extend Lee's line of thinking here to include those ways of thinking central to experiences of trauma; empathizing with characters, for example, is central to reading comprehension in fiction (Rainey, 2017). Building a sense of empathy—for oneself and others—is important for those who have experienced or are experiencing trauma, as empathy is one protective factor against retraumatization and supporting resilience; developing empathy strengthens the ability to understand and relate to others' feelings, perspectives, and experiences. Empathetic people tend to care about how their thoughts, actions, decisions, and words impact how they see themselves and others (Frey et al., 2019). In short, trauma-sensitive literacy instruction involves more than simply asking students to read about students' experiences of trauma. It asks teachers to highlight how students' resilience is helpful academically. In ELA, we are fortunate because resilience is at the heart of the discipline. As one of Britnie's English professors told her, all great literature is ultimately about only one thing: the triumph of the human spirit.

Pillar V: Foster Peer–Peer Relationships That Honor Multiple Perspectives

Our final pillar of trauma-sensitive literacy instruction lies in the power of peer relationships. One of the foremost insights from research on socio-emotional learning—and on learning in general (Bransford et al., 2000)—is the need to build classroom communities where students feel a sense of safety and belonging (O'Drobinak & Kelley, 2021). Indeed, research shows that the effect of positive peer relationships is nearly identical to the effect of positive student–teacher relationships (Hattie, 2018). Perhaps unsurprisingly, feeling disliked by peers has a negative effect (Hattie, 2018). For students who have experienced trauma, being disliked can be incredibly corrosive because students may isolate themselves if they perceive themselves in a negative light, which limits their ability to draw on the protective factors of peer relationships (Fisher et al., 2020). Therefore, educators must teach their students to care about themselves and one another.

Scholars have sought to understand better peer–peer relationships and their effects on life outcomes in terms of social capital, which refers to the resources embedded within and derived from a student's social networks, including their communities, families, schools, and friends (Fisher et al., 2020; Salloum et al., 2017). Social capital is a set of shared values that allows students to collaborate and work together toward a common goal. Students with strong social capital feel emotionally and psychologically safe, leading to a greater sense of agency in their own lives. This is particularly important for students who are experiencing or have experienced trauma; a person's belief in their own "capacity to take action and shape [their] destiny" (Frey et al., 2019, p. 21) is often taken from those experiencing trauma. Students with weak social capital feel less secure and may not attempt to tackle challenges or try new things. Social capital is related to graduation and dropout rates, behavioral interventions, school safety, and academic learning (Bryk et al., 2010; Salloum et al., 2017).

The two most commonly known forms of social capital are bonding and bridging. Bonding capital describes connections among groups and community members with similar demographic characteristics and resources, and bridging capital is between those with different characteristics as measurements and improvement for youth and young adults of color or low-income backgrounds. However, Scales and colleagues (2020) note an unequal distribution when it comes to social capital because these two forms of capital do not fully consider the systemic oppression faced by historically marginalized people. Therefore, students also need linking social capital, which connects and builds relationships between unequal power dynamics, such as positions of authority and teacher–student relationships.

As educators, we need to be aware of all three types of social capital, providing opportunities for students to develop bonding and bridging capital and linking capital, in which students make connections across power and status differences. Therefore, we must devote time and energy to understanding the value of the networks of relationships that students bring with them to school. We highly recommend reading Scales and colleagues' report (2020) to learn more about their framework.

For those interested in learning more about social capital in their classroom, we recommend the Sociogram Maps discussed by Fisher and colleagues (2020), where students ask themselves the following questions:

- Who are three people in this class you would most like to work with in a collaborative learning task?
- Who are three people in this class you would most like to play with at recess? (For older students, ask who they would like to eat lunch with.)
- Who are three people in this class you would most like to meet with for a fun weekend activity? (p. 40)

Groupwork in ELA Classrooms

Of course, we can't discuss peer–peer relationships without discussing collaborative work in classrooms. Evidence continues to mount that providing opportunities for students to work together in groups supports literacy and language development because talking through academic ideas in relatively low-stakes environments supports reading comprehension and language development for mono- and multilingual students alike (e.g., Calderon & Slakk, 2018). These are long-standing findings in adolescent literacy (Jacobs, 2008).

What is less well understood is the potential of collaborative work for students who are experiencing or have experienced trauma. As we have said, trauma is often experienced as shameful, isolating, and marginalizing. To counteract these forces, students need opportunities to bring aspects of themselves and their life experiences into classrooms. This does not mean that students necessarily bring their darkest sadness out for display during a class discussion on Laurie Halse Anderson's 1999 novel *Speak*.

Instead, it means that students have opportunities to work with others as they make deeply felt connections between the concepts, themes, and ideas explored in class and their lives. Through discussions about current events, themes in books, or other ways trauma is discussed and shared in the classroom, we believe that peer relationships can strongly support those who want to share their situations. Students must always have choices about what they share and with whom. Through these informal relationships, students have opportunities to explore shared experiences, talk through the meaning of events, listen to and support one another, and even problem-solve solutions. Throughout our chapters, we will discuss specific ways to organize collaborative work in support of trauma-sensitive literacy instruction. In addition, establishing a positive peer culture can empower students to support one another through experiences of collective trauma or trauma shared by an entire community or population, such as school shootings, hurricanes, or a global pandemic that exposes students to trauma experienced by many (Craig, 2017). This is where trauma-sensitive literacy practices can be a step in supporting students both academically and emotionally.

Of course, not all students will immediately thrive while working in collaborative groups. They may be afraid of the consequences of speaking up—at least initially—or they may be unfamiliar with norms for positive group interaction. If this is the case, students may not experience the power of exploring potential next steps or brainstorming questions they might discuss with trusted adults. Thus, students will need support to develop the skills they need to help each other make deep and cognitively rigorous connections between themes, essential questions, or concepts under study and students' own lives. Therefore, teachers' expectations for how students should interact with each other are clear, and the kinds of discourse valued in class should be modeled for students. For students who have or are currently experiencing trauma, this means that teachers need to model not only how to use academic language to connect claims to evidence, for example, but also that they need to model what it means to share our vulnerabilities and make meaningful connections between literature and life.

CONCLUSION

At the heart of research on students experiencing trauma is the idea that trauma-sensitive instruction should support students in building resilience. As we discussed in Chapter 1, more students than we might first imagine experience trauma in the United States, but not all students experience trauma in the same way. The good news is that what is needed to support students experiencing trauma is within our reach. As educators, we *can* learn about trauma and its potential causes and develop a caring classroom community built on positive relationships. In this chapter, we have zeroed in on a framework through which we can think about how to build trauma-sensitive literacy instruction: We can create caring classrooms by investigating our own biases, promoting students' choices, sharing our vulnerability, building from who students are and what they already know, and fostering peer–peer relationships. In chapters 3 through 6, we show how this framework informs specific aspects of ELA instruction, including curating and selecting texts, leading discussions of literature, teaching writing, and teaching for inquiry. Finally, Chapter 7 discusses common concerns for teachers in trauma-sensitive literacy instruction and teachers' need for self-care.

CHAPTER 3

Curating Appropriate, High-Quality Literature in TSLI

As I (Rachelle) write this chapter, I sit and contemplate my thoughts, feelings, and anger regarding the overturning of *Roe v. Wade*. This decision worries me not only for myself but also for the many young women, nonbinary, and trans students who will walk into my classroom and know they are not safe. They understand that with this decision, the Supreme Court judges have determined that their bodies are no longer their own and that state governments will determine what decisions they are allowed to make and when. As I sit here, I read how various state politicians quickly push their anti-abortion laws, bills previously tabled with the caveat that they would go into full effect if *Roe v. Wade* were overturned. Laws intended to take away the rights, or at the very least, make decisions for others. I worry and want to take action.

I want to understand how one's religious beliefs become grounds for the political decision-making of an entire group of people. I reflect on reading *The Handmaid's Tale* by Margaret Atwood years ago and thinking how scary the world in the book was where women had no say and were considered property. Women were lumped into six groups: handmaids, wives, Marthas, Aunts, Econowives, and Unwomen. They had no say on how they would be identified and had no say over their bodies or lives as they were under the control of men in a patriarchal society. While this is a work of fiction, women today are being treated as property without a voice, without a say in decisions that impact their lives and health, and without care.

And then, I reflect on the words shared by Supreme Court Judge Clarence Thomas, as he casually mentioned a need to investigate other federal decisions related to birth control, same-sex marriage, and other freedoms that all Americans deserve. I ponder what this means for many people in America, and I am perplexed about how our nation has come to this point. However, I also realize that this current action against a group of people is not the first—and probably not the last—where a group of people dictates what others can and cannot do.

As a human, a female human, I want to ensure that teachers I work alongside, and their students, are allowed to process what this means for them and share their thoughts and experiences (always by invitation and never forced). Because at this moment in history, we are experiencing an extreme amount of societal trauma inflicted on *us* by *us*. And a message is being shared and understood by many—guns that lead to mass shootings have more rights than people. At times like this, I want to do three main things: read, become more knowledgeable, and take action.

In an ELA classroom, students read many texts; literature is central to the curriculum. Instruction includes whole-class novels, short stories, poems, and other print-based texts, along with multimodal texts that are becoming more common in ELA classrooms. Multimodal texts—such as picture books, graphic novels, anime, comics, video games, posters, lyrics, artwork, blogs, brochures, and many others—require multiple modes to comprehend and communicate. Students analyze themes and examine the author's structure and word usage choices, among the many other required standards. How we select literature and which stories we include can promote trauma-sensitive literacy instruction or potentially cause traumatic experiences. This chapter focuses predominantly on the novel-based text, with literature at the center—keeping in mind our five pillars for trauma-sensitive literacy instruction framework.

This chapter explores the necessity of selecting inclusive and diverse stories to honor many voices, perspectives, and cultures. As we will discuss, people of color and LGBTQ+ people continue to be underrepresented in fiction and often include stereotypical and negative portrayals. Therefore, we share ideas for curating and incorporating literature in ELA classrooms and curriculum that incorporate voices from historically marginalized groups. We highlight how doing so builds a classroom that focuses on all students' safety in caring ways that promote the cultivation of strong relationships.

WHAT DOES LITERATURE HAVE TO DO WITH IT?

As we know, traumatic experiences can occur at home, on playgrounds, and in schools. Schools have created a prison-like atmosphere to "prevent" school shootings. Unfortunately, these tragedies continue to occur. Systemic oppression continues even as schools implement anti-bullying rules and regulations. LGBTQ+, Black, Brown, Muslim, Indigenous, and many others experience targeted trauma in the real world, via social media, community members, and even classmates (e.g., Alvarez, 2020; Love, 2019; National Child Traumatic Stress Network, Justice Consortium, Schools Committee, and Culture Consortium, 2017). Typically, this is because of how they identify or what they look like, with antiquated and inappropriate messages or recommendations for success—such as, pulling themselves up by the bootstraps—without the necessary resources, support, or understanding of racial and generational trauma. How we respond to the experiences our students face may prompt feelings of shame, humiliation, betrayal, and isolation (Craig, 2017) or may move students toward resilience (Fisher et al., 2020).

Literature can be powerful in trauma-sensitive literacy instruction (TSLI) because it can open dialogue about the traumatic experiences of many students. A central point in this chapter is that readers interact, engage, and learn from what they read based on their lived experiences (Beers & Probst, 2017). Importantly, as educators, we want to choose texts that provide students an opportunity to learn *and* genuinely be motivated and interested in their reading. Otherwise, students may zone out if we present lessons and use novels they can't relate to. The most drastic consequence is when students say they "hate reading." Therefore, literature is one impactful way to support building students' resilience.

For this reason and numerous others, as noted below, many well-written books have been published specifically to support ELA teachers in using all types of novels and genres to bring students into imagined realms and process real-world realities and hardships. These resources provide additional information on creating opportunities for trauma-sensitive literacy instruction by addressing race, class, gender, privilege, trauma, empathy, mental illness, and so much more through stories and expertly written texts. This is wonderful! These authors understand that books serve as a way for students to escape current realities and challenges, explore ways to problem-solve their situations with fictional and real-life people, learn about others' cultures and experiences, and ultimately, develop agency to stand up, speak up, and promote change. As I write this last sentence, I have goosebumps because it's exciting to think how our classrooms can evoke so much support and learning and be catalysts for social justice and action!

Curating and using authentic, diverse novels that create opportunities for students to see themselves and their experiences in what they read and learn about others promotes the development of empathy and action (Hays, 2021; Mirra, 2018). These teachers understand that to address students' emotional needs, they must choose stories that provide mirrors and windows for readers to understand themselves and others (Sims Bishop, 1990). As mirrors, books allow readers to see themselves through the actions, decisions, and dialogue of at least one character. Windows provide a way for students to take meaning from the story, apply it to their lives, develop empathy, and gain knowledge about people unlike themselves. As windows, these narratives allow our students to meet people they otherwise might not have met. Mirrors allow us to recognize the similarities across human experiences and let students know they are not alone. In other words, students can read not only to understand themselves but also to understand the lives of others (Sims Bishop, 1990), witnessing how characters deal with hardships (Rodríguez, 2019).

Recommended Books for Further Learning on Using Literature in the Classroom

- *Breaking the Taboo with Young Adult Literature* edited by V. Malo-Juvera and P. Greathouse.
- *Critical Content Analysis of Children's and Young Adult Literature: Reframing Perspective* edited by H. Johnson, J. Mathis, and K. G. Short.
- *Developing Mathematical Literacy through Adolescent Literature* by P. Greathouse and H. G. Anthony.
- *Engaging Empathy and Activating Agency: Young Adult Literature as a Catalyst for Action* by A. D. Hays.
- *Engaging With Multicultural YA Literature in the Secondary Classroom: Critical Approaches for Critical Education* edited by R. Ginsberg and W. J. Glenn.
- *Expanding the Foundation: African American Authors of Young Adult Literature, 1980–2000* edited by S. T. Bickmore and S. P. Clark.
- *Fostering Mental Health Literacy through Adolescent Literature* edited by B. Eisenbach and J. S. Frydman.
- *Letting Go of Literary Whiteness: Anti-racist Literature Instruction for White Students* by C. Borsheim-Black and S. T. Sarigiandes.
- *Teaching Culturally Sustaining and Inclusive Young Adult Literature: Critical Perspectives and Conversations* by R. J. Rodríguez.
- *Teaching Reading with YA Literature: Complex Texts, Complex Lives* by Jennifer Buehler.
- *Teaching the "Taboo": Diverse and Inclusive Literature Is the Way* edited by R. S. Savitz, L. Roberts, and J. DeHart.

Using mirrors and windows, literature can foster safe classrooms where all students belong and are welcomed regardless of who they are and what they have experienced. By being intentional, teachers choose novels that provide an opportunity to teach the required standards *and* build and reinforce relationships among students—meaning they do not rely solely on the often-used classics. These teachers disrupt the hidden curriculum narrative too often present in our ELA classrooms.

Overcoming the Hidden Curriculum as TSLI

An English Language Arts classroom tends to focus on using the literary canon. And often, when we ask teachers why they lean toward these classic novels, the number one reason is that doing so exposes students to the world's great ideas. Another oft-mentioned reason is that the canon is part of the content-knowledge of ELA (as in, you can't be an educated person if you haven't read Shakespeare). This is an alarming reason, but it has been part of the ELA landscape for decades (Hirsh, 1987). Another common reason is that they fell in love with these books as students.

However, making canonical literature a dominant focus of the formal curriculum communicates much more than the tales of two European cities. Students might learn to analyze literature through the lens of Victorian England (or Elizabethan English or American expatriates living in Paris in the 1920s). However, students also learn a set of implicit lessons: The world's so-called "great" ideas have a heritage that is almost exclusively white, predominantly male, heterosexual (at least in appearance), and Christian (Borsheim-Black et al., 2014; Borsheim-Black, 2015). As a 3rd-grade classroom teacher, John Byrd recently shared with us the need to choose what we share in our classrooms intentionally:

> Our curriculum is written through a European American lens, and the experiences and history of other races are ignored or treated as supporting characters. Our curriculum does not consciously choose to highlight the work that other cultures have brought forth to society, and this has lasting effects. When students do not see themselves reflected, they become disinterested, and when this happens, it leads to failing grades, misbehavior, and eventually dropping out.

Therefore, for most of our students, the messages sent are loud and grating: Your people did not contribute to the world's great ideas. This representation of things is, first and foremost, a farce since it willfully ignores the outstanding contributions of so many cultures and individuals. It also profoundly damages our students' views of their ancestors' contributions to academic life and, by extension, their perceptions of their potential to be contributing members of intellectual communities. In short, the hidden curriculum can be profoundly damaging and even traumatic for students because it is a powerful conduit through which the implicit biases of societies and individuals communicated in schools.

Elizabeth Dutro's (2019) work elegantly points out the damage that the hidden curriculum can do, particularly for students who have experienced trauma in ways that are not normative to middle-class, white society in the United States. In a 2010 case study, Dutro outlines a classroom in which the day's story—featured in a textbook—described a middle-class community in which people pooled their resources and helped one another after experiencing a natural disaster. On its face, the story was a sweet little tale about the power of communal living. However, Dutro's analysis peels back the layers of this assumption, revealing the biases hidden within the textbook's presentation of this story. As Dutro (2010) points out, the textbook's questions were presumably intended to support students in making personal connections to the story since they asked students about a time when their community had experienced hardship and how their communities had come together to surmount that challenge. However, Dutro highlights that these seemingly innocuous questions assume that communities have resources to share and that hard work can overcome adversity. These assumptions can be harmful from both an intellectual and an affective standpoint since they overlook generational poverty's influence and only present the standpoint from the middle-class perspective. They can be harmful because they fail to represent the lived experiences of those growing up outside the middle class. These middle-class assumptions permeate school-based interpretations of stories, and these assumptions can over-simplify students' experiences of trauma—their lived experiences. While generally implicit, this perspective is still alive and well in schools today, as we explore in the next section on book banning *and* how the political climate or personal beliefs prompt self-censorship.

Banning of Books

Calls for book bans and political policies to ban books have skyrocketed over the past couple of years. Nationwide, parents, school board members, politicians, and others have mobilized and called for the extensive banning of books in classrooms and school/public libraries. *The New York Times* reported in April 2022 that "attempts to ban books in the United States surged in 2021 to the highest level since the American Library Association began tracking book challenges 20 years ago" (Harris & Alter, 2022, n.p.). *The Washington Post* stated that we are now "seeing a new wave of book bans, marked by an unprecedented number of challenges and intense polarization" focused on narrowing the availability of books that "might challenge young people on [topics related to] race and gender—the same issues at the center of the political and cultural wars ripping through the country" (Strauss, 2022). These sources and others (e.g., Natanson, 2022) draw on the American Library Association's (ALA) annual report on censorship, a document that notes 729 attempts to remove books from public libraries, schools, and universities in 2021 and 1,597 challenges of books and removals of books.

The ALA compiles an annual list of the Top 10 Most Challenged Books, which includes the provided justifications for each challenged novel. In 2021 (www.ala.org/advocacy/bbooks/frequentlychallengedbooks/top10), the top five most challenged books were

1. *Gender Queer* by Maia Kobabe
   Reasons: Banned, challenged, and restricted for LGBTQIA+ content; sexually explicit images
2. *Lawn Boy* by Jonathan Evison
   Reasons: Banned and challenged for LGBTQIA+ content; sexually explicit messages

3. *All Boys Aren't Blue* by George M. Johnson
   Reasons: Banned and challenged for LGBTQIA+ content; profanity; sexual explicitness
4. *Out of Darkness* by Ashley Hope Perez
   Reasons: Banned, challenged, and restricted for depictions of abuse; sexual explicitness
5. *The Hate U Give* by Angie Thomas
   Reasons: Banned and challenged for profanity; violence; anti-police messages; and indoctrination of a social agenda

As you may have noticed, many banned and challenged books depicted people of color and members of the LGBTQ+ community, among other intersections of identity. The striking tendency of book bans to target titles written by and featuring people of color and members of the LGBTQ+ community is difficult to ignore.

Additionally, across much of America, laws have recently been passed restricting how and whether teachers can select, assign, and discuss these books (Savitz et al., 2023). Sometimes teachers must choose between their jobs *or* advocating and using inclusive practices that value all students and their lived experiences. In other words, these laws tell teachers they must not discuss race, gender, or sexuality. For instance, teachers that I (Rachelle) work with from Tennessee have called to ask for advice after the legislature passed a law that prohibits teachers from saying that any individual is inherently racist due to their race or that individuals are responsible for actions taken by members of their race in the past. This led one school district and parents in that community to challenge an autobiography of Ruby Bridges. They reasoned that it violated the state's law by teaching that "white people are bad" and "America is unjust." Another well-known law is the Florida ruling, now renamed the "Don't Say Gay" law, which explicitly states that books about sexual orientation and gender identity cannot be included in many classrooms and instruction, leaving teachers unsure what will happen if they include stories that represent all their students and community members.

Unfortunately, these laws and policies impact publishers, too, as they must decide if they will advocate against these harmful laws, knowing that some of these states control most textbook purchasing, *or* stand up against these destructive, dangerous, and exclusive policies. For instance, recently, well-known equity scholars have broken their book contracts and speaking engagements with one publisher because the publisher chose not to stand up for equity: the publisher decided to modify a standard elementary reading curriculum to pull any mention of inclusion, race, or other historically and contemporarily marginalized populations (Goldstein, 2022).

The irony is that all this comes when white characters still dominate children's literature and stories published in textbooks. Characters of color are underrepresented compared to the demographics of youth across America. According to the data on books by and about Black, Indigenous, and People of Color published for children and teens compiled by the Cooperative Children's Book Center, School of Education, University of Wisconsin–Madison (2021), of the 3,183 books sent by publishers for review since 2018, very few are written by or about people of color. For instance, the highest percentage category for authorship is 15% written by Asian authors, followed by 10% Black/African, and 10% Latinx, with a swift drop to 1% or less for Indigenous, Pacific Islanders, or Arab-identifying authors. The numbers are similar for books about or inclusive of characters of color, with the highest representation at 14% for Black/African, followed by 11% Asian, dropping to 7% for Latinx, and then less than 1% for Indigenous, Pacific Islander, and Arab character representation. If you want to find a specific topic or representation, there is a diversity statistics book search that includes diversity filters and time frames; it also includes a list of reviewed books and recommendations (ccbc.education.wisc.edu/diversity-statistics-book-search).

We ask you now to stop and think about your curricula to consider what books are most valued in your classroom. How many classics are included, and do they contain harmful narratives about historically marginalized groups? Do they inaccurately portray traumatic experiences? What diversity is presented in your classroom library, and how much is perceived as inclusivity? Are the district-required curricula inclusive? These are important questions to ask! Here's why.

Amanda Rigell and her colleagues (2022) conducted a qualitative analysis of a scripted K–8 English Language Arts curriculum called *Wit and Wisdom*. They investigated how this curriculum reproduces a white supremacist stance. Following an analysis of racial representation across all core and supplementary texts in the curriculum, they further analyzed these materials by grade level. What they found, which may surprise some of you, was that whiteness was centered in every aspect of this curriculum—from the chosen texts, how stories were grouped, and even within the scripted lessons teachers were to use to teach these novels. They found the erasure of all non-white people in the lower elementary-grade materials with a similar exclusion in the upper elementary grades except for the inclusion of Black, Indigenous, People of Color (BIPOC) when discussing "'cultural conflict,' 'breaking barriers,' art, and immigration" (p. 7). As Rigell and her colleagues noted, these materials exclude BIPOC characters or representations from units of "scientific exploration, courage and persistence, and domestic and foreign wars that fundamentally shaped US history" (p. 7).

For the middle-grade units, the curricula seemingly avoided discussion about race even when the lessons were about the racist history of the United States, such as the Civil Rights Movement. Too often, curricula like these only teach harmful and inaccurate narratives of BIPOC and lack the ability for students to explore and investigate oppression and to value their lived experiences and histories. They perpetuate stereotypes of people, races, and ethnicities, and are not authentic or representative.

Let's take a moment to explore what this means. Often, when we see characters identified as Indigenous People, they are described as aggressive. Alternatively, we read about the stereotype of a Black family whose missing father figure is incarcerated for drugs or gang life. Another common issue is when cultural traditions and customs are written as though all members of a cultural group participate in the same cultural practices. For example, one assumption is that all Hispanic and Latinx people celebrate Cinco de Mayo as Independence Day versus knowing it commemorates a single battle. As you may imagine, this could be traumatic for students who need to see their identities represented positively, only to find these false and dangerous narratives. We recommend taking a moment to think through some of the fiction you have used over the past year or so—are there generalizations and stereotypes presented? If so, how was instruction incorporated to disrupt this problematic issue?

By this point in the chapter, it is clear that classrooms need to contain multifaceted, positive, authentic, and affirming depictions related to race, ethnicity, national origin, family structure, community life, and the list can go on and on. Of course, it takes a lot of time and effort to read through stacks of books and analyze each to determine harmful stereotypes and inaccurate portrayals of people. It is also challenging to ensure that texts include representation across all genres and positive portrayals such as Black joy and Black excellence instead of the constant use of victim narratives. So . . . what can be done? While we do not have all the answers, we offer a few.

What You Can Do—Evaluating Your Classroom Library and Curricula

As mentioned, an excellent first step is to evaluate the texts you use for instruction. To do so, we recommend the New York University Metropolitan Center for Research on Equity and the Transformation of Schools (2019) *Culturally Responsive Curriculum Scorecard*. As shared on their website (steinhardt.nyu.edu/metrocenter/ejroc/services/culturally-responsive-curriculum-scorecards), this scorecard was collaboratively developed with NYC parents, students, educators, and researchers as a tool to help determine the extent to which English Language Arts, Science, Technology, Engineering, Arts, and Mathematics (STEAM) curricula are (or are not) culturally responsive and sustaining. The scorecard allows teachers to customize based on context and the conditions at their school. They provide educators with seven steps to complete the scorecard and analyze it to determine results with much greater detail and specific instructions on their website. This evaluation has questions to help analyze authenticity—some books labeled as multicultural emphasize the assimilation of dominant narratives (Yoon et al., 2010) and do not endorse positive or accurate narratives (Morrell,

2007). The scorecard has been a game-changer for many teachers we work with each semester.

Another possibility is for students to work together to evaluate character representation in a story, especially about intersecting identities. Donovan and Toliver (2019) provide excellent questions for students to analyze the representation of people:

- Is some aspect of the protagonist's identity positioned as the main conflict?
- How does a character's identity group impact the way others see them?
- What does the character want others to see or understand about themselves and is it centered on some aspect of their identity groups?
- How has a character's history—the family history, identity group history, geopolitical history—created this complex individual?
- Which identity groups are represented as main and supporting characters? Which are not? Why?
- Is there some element of instruction or didacticism about a certain group coming from the author's presentation of one or intersecting identity groups that is stereotypical or is it more nuanced? (p. 89)

What You Can Do—Fight Censorship

Luckily, many organizations, parents, media specialists, students, and even school boards are fighting against censorship laws. Interestingly, this past June marked the 40th anniversary of Steven Pico's legal fight after school officials in New York removed 11 books from the library (Chavez, 2022). With the ACLU, Pico took his case (*Board of Education, Island Trees Union Free School District v. Pico*) to the Supreme Court, where the ruling stated, "school boards may not remove books because they dislike the ideas contained in those titles," citing the First Amendment. Are you surprised to learn of this case and what it means in current book-banning times?

Pushback like this is happening today, too. Yes, there are advocates successfully fighting and preventing the banning of books. For instance, two students in Missouri sued Wentzville School District for violating their civil rights when they banned books from their school libraries. These students, backed by the American Civil Liberties Union (ACLU) of Missouri, prompted the school board to keep one of the challenged books, reversing their initial vote to remove them (Bernhard, 2022).

Similarly, the Kent School Board in Washington voted not to ban a challenged middle school book from middle school libraries after the ACLU of Washington threatened legal action if the book was removed (Greenberg, 2022). In Texas, a group of school librarians fought back by creating a website and swag that stated, "I support #FReadom," a larger movement of Texans resisting efforts to challenge and ban books. This group of librarians used their voices by consistently sending a barrage of messages to Texas lawmakers (Montgomery, 2022). In Florida, Stephana Ferrell, mother of two elementary-age children, advocated against book banning when she organized and campaigned with parents all over the state to stand against censorship. She created the Florida Freedom to Read Project, where she continues to use her voice, along with other parents, to let community members know what is occurring in their local schools, such as new labeling on books as an "advisory notice" to warn the potential reader that community members deemed the book as unsuitable for students (Yurcaba, 2022).

In addition, organizations explicitly geared toward English Language Arts teachers are also speaking out and back. For instance, the National Council of Teachers of English (NCTE) wrote a position statement in 2018 titled "The Students' Right to Read." This statement emphasized their firm position that censorship is problematic. One issue they discuss is how ELA teachers must have the ability to select books that "do not hide, or lie" to the readers "about the perilous but wondrous times we live in, books which talk of the fears, hopes, joys, and frustrations people experience, books about people not only as they are but as they can be" (n.p.). In other words, using books that represent students' lived experiences in the present, past, and future and exploring stories that are complex and potentially difficult to read but relatable to what our students are experiencing. Students must have a choice to read a story that connects with their hardship and reality or to choose a novel that can allow them to learn about someone else's choices and situations.

This organization and this position statement connect what happens when censorship bans become prominent. It is a great resource to read for specific action steps—at the community, school, classroom, and educator levels. They also offer a form that teachers can use to request reconsideration of a banned text. On their Intellectual Freedom Center website (ncte.org/resources/ncte-intellectual-freedom-center), NCTE includes guidance, tools, and support for teachers dealing with book challenges, such as reporting censorship, their rationale database to support challenged books, and ways to stay up to date on current news and research.

Similarly, the International Literacy Association (ILA; 2019) published its position statement, Children's Rights to Excellent Literacy Instruction, advocating "for the right to excellent literacy instruction for children worldwide, which builds on the ten principles in ILA's Children's Rights to Read campaign: ensuring that every child, everywhere, has access to the education, opportunities, and resources needed to read" (p. 1). ILA asserts that literacy and equitable literacy instruction are fundamental human rights. The organization provides additional resources for fighting censorship on their *Children's Rights to Read* website, along with a resolution for educators to sign stating that they adopt the *Children's Rights to Read* in their school, district, or community (literacyworldwide.org/get-resources/childrens-rights-to-read).

Finally, the National Coalition Against Censorship, created with NCTE, provides a handbook for educators to use as a guide when dealing with book challenges in their classrooms (ncac.org/resource/educator-handbook). The ALA has a tool to report challenged books (ala.org/tools/challengesupport/report#:~:text=If%20you%20would%20like%20to,email%20oif%40ala.org). In short, these resources and these stories of individual and collective advocacy highlight that we can work together to fight censorship. Doing so can support all students, including those experiencing trauma.

What You Can Do—Disrupt Self-Censorship

Another consideration at the personal level is a reflection on self-censorship—when teachers use only books that feel safe in their teaching, such as pulling books from classroom and school libraries, not even displaying questioned books. This makes sense when we consider how teachers face punitive action when using books others deem inappropriate. Plus, many may worry about using books that focus on traumatic experiences or are complex—we understand! However, we also know that students are drawn to these heavy topics often deemed "taboo" (Ivey & Johnston, 2018; Savitz et al., 2023). Books are often their go-to initial source for exploring these challenging topics (Gallo & Herrmann, 2018; Savitz et al., 2021).

In 2016, the School Library Journal Research published their findings on self-censorship among school librarians; 90% of elementary and middle school and 73% of high school librarians reported not purchasing a book because it contained controversial topics. The number one reason was that librarians deemed particular books to have "non–age appropriate content" (p. 2). The report found that 12% of middle and 6% of high school libraries have restricted book sections, and 81% of public schools have a policy that provides the procedures for anyone to file a formal book challenge. Four in 10 school librarians report that they dealt with book challenges. While these statistics are a few years old, they still represent the current realities of many school librarians pushed to self-censor when purchasing books or collaborating with others.

Dr. April Leach is a middle school media specialist/librarian in Florida, where she battles state censorship laws daily. She shares about the book review process at her school and, more importantly, her thoughts on why she is walking the fine line to support students when there are problematic laws.

> The South Florida school district where I am a Middle School Media Specialist/Librarian has a book review process to address both book selections and books that may be objectionable to parents or the public. Our district has not had many books submitted for the process,

mainly because one of the first questions that must be answered in the affirmative is whether the person submitting the book for possible removal from library or classroom bookshelves has read the book in its entirety. Under Florida House Bill 1467, we teachers should not utilize books that indoctrinate or persuade students to a particular point of view; however, the language is quite vague.

Last spring, librarians were asked to remove several books from the shelves and bring the books to our principals, including the children's version of the 1619 Project, *Born on the Water* by Nikole Hannah Jones, which I believe is beautifully written and illustrated and vital to include in our library because we are a diverse school with a 28% Haitian Creole and African American population. This semester the district has made it mandatory for all book purchases for school libraries to be made by Certified Media Specialists. This sounds perfectly reasonable; however, not all schools have certified media specialists due to a severe teacher shortage and choices made by principals and administrators, which presents an obstacle for some schools. Furthermore, every book must have two independent professional reviews. We are provided a list of such reviewers as well as a reviewed book database and a Books with No Reviews Justification Form to fill out. For all book purchases, we must submit a list and then wait 2 weeks before purchasing or accepting donations. Even then, this fall, the book previously mentioned being pulled was allowed to be placed back on our shelves, revealing mixed signals from the state regarding how decisions are made about book banning.

Decisions I make about purchasing books at the 6–8 grade level for my population of 80% English language learners are determined by student interest, reading levels, and what the content area teachers are presenting in their curricula. A majority of our students want to read graphic novels; those are the books that circulate the most, so that is what I have been making available and writing grants to be able to expand our collection.

Because many students at my middle school are questioning their gender identity and sexual orientation, as well as forming world views, I try to make available books that answer questions and support the decisions these students are making about themselves that help yet do not indoctrinate or persuade. This is a fine line, but I do this because it is my perception that in times of conservative repression of fundamental freedoms guaranteed by our Constitution, it is my job as an educator to provide tools students need to think for themselves and to support an empathetic mindset. As future problem-solvers in a world that we are bequeathing fraught with major local and global issues, we owe students our very best models of standing for what is right, notwithstanding pressures from those who do not share this worldview.

As you will read in the remaining pages of this chapter, when we move past our discomfort and become intentional about the books we buy and use in our classrooms, like what Dr. Leach is doing, we invite all students to live and learn in our ELA classrooms. Therefore, as educators, we can choose to nurture and develop social competence by creating a classroom surrounded by care and understanding that our students are represented and included in our curriculum and instruction—a protective factor important for students experiencing trauma.

The following section is crucial for educators who care about students and who work hard to establish collaborative and positive peer engagement and include diverse novels in our classrooms. So, here comes the fun part—let's talk books, novels, and ways to embed stories throughout an ELA lesson, unit, and the school year.

CURATING NOVELS TO BUILD CLASSROOM LIBRARIES

When we build classrooms upon respect, safety, and belonging, students want to read what we read. When we self-censor or shy away from using novels that are relevant to students' lives or topics because they are considered "taboo" (Savitz et al., 2023), our ELA instruction can become centered on a dominant narrative, undermining and silencing the complex and diverse experiences of our entire student population (Nieto & Bode, 2018). Teaching these "taboo" topics is a crucial way to address trauma and normalize these conversations with students (Ayers & Ayers, 2014; Dutro, 2019) because literature can promote students' development of empathy as they learn to understand their preexisting beliefs and assumptions and to learn from others' perspectives (Fisher et al., 2020; Ivey & Johnston, 2018; Mirra, 2018; Turner & Reed, 2018).

Helping students in this way influences their identities, particularly their perception of themselves and their attributes and talents compared to others (Frey et al., 2019). Using high-quality, authentic, diverse texts is about constructing school and classroom experiences "on a base of fearless and relentless inquiry" (Ayers & Ayers, 2014, p. 2), prompting students and teachers to ask *why*. Why are particular perspectives not included in the text? Whose voices are missing? Ultimately, why do we not discuss adversity, hardships, and traumatic experiences in our classrooms (Savitz & Stockwell, 2021)? Suppose teachers encourage their students to be critical problem posers (Janks, 2010), where they question and analyze the plot and the author's intent and biases as they read, which is discussed more in Chapter 4. In that case, students might ask these questions (or more profound, more personal ones). Their questions might bring up "taboo" topics related to gender identity and sexual orientation, or about abortion, rape culture, teen pregnancy, and even how privilege impacts the socially constructed nature of race and racism (e.g., Delgado & Stefancic, 2017).

Teachers and students need to understand how many students are impacted by traumatic experiences such as domestic violence and bullying and then learn ways to address, cope with, and dismantle the situation. Fisher and colleagues (2020) noted that literature provides an avenue for students to read about problems they may experience through the characters' eyes. As they read, students discover ways that fictional characters deal with their circumstances—reading specific choices and actions taken to solve their issues, finding resources or help, and building resiliency. Reading about traumatic experiences provides a discrete way to explore their situations individually and secretly or by sharing and discussing with others.

One character's experiences, choices, and actions will not replicate what our students face. Therefore, we must provide books that not only cover a gamut of topics and experiences that students regularly face—they must also cover various realities and endings. For instance, several teachers in one of Rachelle's young adult literature classes recently commented on the need to share many and multiple book choices when discussing the topics of asylum seekers, refugees, and immigration. As they noted, our students' experiences are not identical, and if we want to include our students' stories and lives, then we need ample representation, not generalized representations of similar situations.

We now share some ways that we curate stories and select trauma-sensitive literature that provide students with opportunities to connect with characters experiencing their realities and ways for students to learn about the lived situations their peers face. The next section first provides ideas for using book award lists and social media to find and select texts and stories that support a trauma-sensitive literacy classroom.

Finding High-Quality Novels—Award Lists

As shared by Fisher and colleagues (2020), many organizations publish annual book recommendation book lists, such as ILA's Young Adult Choices lists (literacyworldwide.org/get-resources/reading-lists). The Assembly on Literature for Adolescents of NCTE has numerous awards, such as the Amelia Elizabeth Walden Book Award for Young Adult Fiction (alan-ya.org/awards/walden-award) and an Award for Excellence in Poetry for Children (ncte.org/awards/excellence-in-poetry-for-children-living-american-poet). It also has a teacher-friendly resource that we highly recommend called Build Your Stack (ncte.org/build-your-stack). Here, teachers can find ELA teacher–curated book lists and options based on specific topics, such as size diversity, hope and humanity, and grief, in addition to culturally affirming books. Teachers even post where they go to find books and how the author matches books with students. What a great resource as we build our classroom libraries!

Another excellent resource for finding award-winning books is ALA's many awards (ala.org/awardsgrants/awards), such as the Schneider Family Book Award, the Coretta Scott King Book Award, the Pura Belpré Award, and the Asian/Pacific American Award, among others. Others include the Whippoorwill Book Award for Rural Young Adult Literature (guides.library.unk.edu/c.php?g=510618&p=7674895), the Jhalak Prize (jhalakprize.com), and the Joan F Kaywell Books Save Lives Award (lib.usf.edu/special-collections/tampa/childrens-young-adult-literature/hipple/kaywell-award).

Finding High-Quality Novels—Social Media

Okay, now you have lots of places to find a variety of award-winning novels; the next consideration is for those who are social media savvy. While there are many excellent personal and organizational hashtags and great Twitter and Facebook pages, we explore a few of our favorites. However, we recommend also asking your colleagues, teacher friends, and students about their go-to places.

Let's first explore some hashtags that we recommend. One popular and well-known hashtag is #weneeddiversebooks. The organizers of this tag (diversebooks.org) share on their home page to "Imagine a world in which all children can see themselves in the pages of a book." They also have already curated diverse book subscription boxes, ways to engage with other educators, and a way to submit a proposal for purchasing diverse book grants!

Another go-to hashtag is #disrupttexts. This crowd-sourced effort is by teachers for teachers with the intent to challenge the traditional literary canon to "create a more inclusive, representative, and equitable language arts curriculum" for all students (disrupttexts.org). Other hashtags you may want to explore are #readwithpride, #AdLit, #YALit, #Goodreads, and #bookaddict, along with Twitter handles and Facebook pages for the previously mentioned organizations.

One of Rachelle's favorite Facebook groups and blog forums is *A Mighty Girl*. The day after the overturning of *Roe v. Wade*, as I wrote the introduction of this chapter, I found inspiration. On June 24, Katherine, a blog writer for this forum, wrote a post entitled, *Dissent Is Patriotic: 50 Books about Girls and Women Who Fought for Change*. Posts like this share book options that spotlight how girls and women fight for various causes and advance science. These books empowered me as I read, and they will do the same for you and your students.

As Brittany Raymond shared, there is "incredible power in reading literature that aligns with the hurts you have endured, and there is even greater strength to be gained in enabling a voice to share these hurts" (2021, p. 72). Our chosen novels for instruction need to resonate with our students' experiences to promote the ability to build upon protective factors and to lead toward resilience when they see their experiences validated in what they read (Anderson, 2019). Therefore, it is essential to do what is possible to curate an extensive classroom library (or frequent visits to the school library) full of all genres and myriad representations of varying cultures, identities, and ethnicities, and a variety of exposition, fiction, poetry, and more.

Sharing Your New Books With Students

Okay, you now have new book options you want to share with your students. Another question we hear often is, How do I introduce these excellent novels to my students when my teaching time is so limited? A great start is to wonder—and then to wander. How do you find new books to read? Do you read book reviews? Do you seek recommendations from friends and colleagues? Do you like one book and then seek out others by the same author? These techniques all work well, and they probably align with how students decide which books they want to read.

For instance, in my (Rachelle) classroom, I took the first few minutes to read aloud a few pages of various books at the start of class. At times, I would read the first few pages, and other times, I would find dramatic or pivotal points in a story and read those pages. The goal was to pique students' interest and spark their curiosity—build motivation to read these books.

After these readings, I ensured the books were visible, along with others, all over the classroom. Books were stacked on my desk; the chalk tray was full of books. Books lined almost all flat surfaces. I moved books around each week and added new books when students checked out titles. I also shared my recommendations with them.

As students read their chosen books, they shared their recommendations. One wall was devoted to this—students wrote the title, author, and their thoughts on little bulletin board book cutouts and then placed them on the wall for all to see. Importantly, students were allowed to remain anonymous if they chose. As students found books they wanted to read, they signed up to grab the book next—although it helps to have multiple copies of well-loved titles. Students also requested book purchases, and I did my best to honor their requests by purchasing what they were craving—writing grant proposals to businesses like Dollar General and previously mentioned literacy organizations that offer to fund teachers to build classroom libraries. I also sought school and district funding and researched literacy scholars and experts who provided scholarships and funding to purchase books. What an incredible moment when students started the year claiming they don't read (in reality, they hadn't found a book they liked—just yet), and soon, they began asking for books, realizing that I valued their input and wanted to honor *their* choices.

Another option for introducing new titles to students is called a book tasting. Let's peek into Debbie Myers's 6th-Grade Reading classroom as she describes what a book tasting is and how she uses them in her classroom.

> A book tasting is dedicated to learning a little bit more about many different books. Think about a wine tasting or ordering a flight of soup. The taster gets to sample a whole bunch in one sitting. In this case, the readers are sampling books, and I will soon want them to "taste" books that are windows, mirrors, and sliding glass doors.
>
> Like many other teachers, I greet my students in the hall on the first day of school. What might set me apart from other teachers is that in my arms, I am holding the stack of books I read over the summer. I work through the stack of books, and I explain how each one allowed me to live a similar life, see into someone else's experience, or go to an entirely different world. And then, I explain how it's important for them to do the same thing as readers. I explain that it's vital to their growth as humans to see they are not alone in the experiences they have lived and continue to live, including the traumas each face. I also want them to learn from experiences outside of the ones they've lived, to know that there are whole other worlds out there and that through reading the words on the pages, they can escape from this one when life gets to be a bit much.
>
> Over the next couple of days, my readers and I will learn to taste books to curate to-be-read piles for ourselves. We work together to create random stacks of books (about 5 to 8 books in each stack), and then each reader will "taste" their stack to determine books that are mirrors, windows, and sliding glass doors. I start by suggesting they spend time checking out the front cover, reading the inside flap, reading the back cover, and then reading the first 3 to 5 pages to get an idea of what the book might be about.
>
> This procedure is how I typically taste a book, but over the years, I've learned that readers prefer to taste books in their ways. I must be okay with this and let them engage how they see fit as they learn what works for them. For instance, last year, I had a reader who tasted books by skipping around to random pages and reading a paragraph here and there. I had another reader who read the entire last chapter to decide if she was interested in reading the whole book. For me, the only "must happen" in a tasting is that each reader curates a pile of at least three books—and I'd love for those books to be one window, one mirror, and one sliding glass door—but I'm also okay if that does not happen. They will get there. I promise they will if we give them time and space to get there.

> It is important to understand that book tastings occur at the start of the year—and then again throughout the year as this activity engages and motivates students in ways that no other reading activity can. In fact, it's not unusual for my students to read over 40 books in a year—not because I forced them, but because they chose them. Through each tasting, they realized how books did not taste all that bad, which prompted them to devour their chosen book and many others.

By sharing pieces about the book with her students, Debbie could pique their interest and motivate them to pick up a new book to read. This may be a strategy you want to try to introduce books to your students so that they engage in individual pleasure reading. However, let's face it: Most of our ELA classroom time relates to required books and stories. Often, teachers we work with share how most books are "chosen" by grade level, providing little room for teacher choice or autonomy. We understand this is a potential barrier, but there are options! We next explore anchor texts and text sets.

Canonical and Middle Grades/Young Adult Literature Pairings

We understand that ELA teachers often use certain novels from the literary canon or district-provided lists. And we agree that many of these books are well written, contain helpful tidbits, and support learning specific techniques and themes. Right now, you may be thinking of your passion for teaching *Romeo and Juliet* and how you create instruction to connect their tragic love story with modern life and students' personal lives. This play is an excellent option, one of many that can prompt discussion about traumatic experiences such as suicide, pressure from outside sources, and hardships. As we have mentioned, connection and authenticity are musts in trauma-sensitive classrooms.

Yet, reading this play can be confusing for many students, especially if they do not have guidance on reading the words, are required to have a single interpretation of Shakespeare's elegant phrasing, or struggle to connect to the time period. Therefore, if we want to ensure that all students are part of learning in our classrooms, we must consider ways to support or supplement the canonical texts we teach.

This is where we can use anchor texts. An anchor text is the central text of a lesson or unit. It can take any form of text, such as another novel, short story, informational text, image, video, or multimodal option. Traditionally, the anchor text is assigned within district-created lessons and is aligned with required state standards. This also means that it is often at the grade level and not the reading level for all learners. Or, as was true in Britnie's class, the anchor text did not come with a district-created lesson plan or unit. It was not aligned with state standards and was not correlated to students' reading levels. Some of this could have been helpful. Instead, they just threw *The Odyssey* at her and told her to teach it during the third quarter. The point is: A high-quality anchor text requires multiple examinations and extensive close reading to allow students time to investigate, explore, and build curiosity about the various themes and plots. If you are required to teach certain (typically canonical) texts, you can generally use them as anchor texts.

To determine what makes up the text set, additional texts, and stories connected to the theme or topic discussed, you want to determine students' background knowledge and interest related to the novel and any other information that will be part of the upcoming unit. For instance, we share in Chapter 4 how to use Anticipation Guides to ask students open-ended questions related to the theme or other elements of the story to get them thinking ahead about what they will read. Through this discussion, teachers can determine students' perspectives, initial beliefs about the topic, and potential harmful assumptions requiring more information before reading. These discussions allow teachers to formatively assess students' understanding and determine how and when to incorporate additional scaffolds and supports for students.

As you build your text set, you want to consider how students can and cannot connect to the whole-class story. Some students may prefer digging into similar themes and concepts first with other types of texts. For instance, there are plenty of tragic love songs that students can explore and analyze before or while reading Shakespeare. Some students may want to explore the themes through artwork and pictures. Others may need more information on the characters and setting of the storyline. And some might benefit from reading a more recent version of this love story. Therefore, text sets could include all types of text, including music, art, spoken word, pictures, and any version of oral, print, or multimodal text that connects to the theme or concept of the unit.

Right now, you may be shaking your head, wondering why teaching with text sets is a good idea when it can be a struggle to get through just one text with your students. Reading multiple texts across a topic or theme promotes students' analysis of similarities and differences across texts (Batchelor, 2018), evaluating whose perspectives are included and whose voices are missing or silenced. Adding texts requires students to engage with diverse perspectives, experiences, and stories, which pushes students past learning a single-story narrative (Adichie, 2009). Text sets provide an opportunity for critical collaborative dialogue, leading students to dive deeper into understanding controversial and complex social issues (Fisher et al., 2020). These necessary skills taught in ELA classrooms align with the required state standards addressing synthesis and learning across multiple texts.

Every chosen text must have a purpose in creating a text set. It sometimes requires us to take a step back and reflect on the objectives of the lessons and the unit to decide how what *we* want aligns with what *students* want, in addition to determining if we are connecting learning to students' interests and experiences. Then, and only then, can we design instruction that uses required texts to center students as part of the curriculum.

Literature Circles

Literature circles are another option to engage students with literature in trauma-sensitive literacy classrooms and in a way that offers students choice in what they read. Through literature, students learn and grow as they experience the protagonist's situations, and students extend their learning through critical dialogue with one another. Literature circles are one way to integrate student-centered reading, learning, and discussion within the classroom (Daniels, 2002). Depending on the literature circle set-up, student groups can read and interact together during class, or groups can establish at-home reading requirements to discuss once they get back together. Either way, group members collaboratively interact with a book or a text set and are often provided support to engage in critical thinking and reflection as they read. Discussion of this type will be further described in Chapter 4.

To set up literature circles, you will first curate a text set of five to eight books for a common theme. Then spend one class period conducting a book pass (Fisher et al., 2020), guiding students to preview each book. A book pass starts with each student having a piece of paper on which they can write the book title and author for each book. Then, students choose their first book to preview, and the teacher provides between 3 to 5 minutes for the student to independently peruse the book. Students may read the back cover, start with page 1, choose somewhere in the middle of the book, or wherever they want to read during the allotted time. When time is up, students rate their interest in each book, sharing additional comments in provided space, such as having already read the book or explaining why they are not interested in reading the book. Typical ratings are 1 (did not want to read) to 5 (wants to read). Once students have had a few minutes to write their comments and share their ratings, they pass their book to another person. The process then repeats with the next book. This type of book pass works best if students are placed into pods so they can easily pass each book around their group.

Taking their ratings and your knowledge of your students, such as how they work with other classmates, create small groups based on student-identified top options. It is essential to share that every book is independently rated, so they may have multiple books with high ratings. Doing so helps place students into groups based on the book option they are excited to read. Once groups are decided, they meet on a regular and predictable schedule, taking on various rotating roles to engage the group while reading. We recommend reading Daniels's *Literature Circles: Voice and Choice in Book Clubs & Reading Groups* (2002) and his co-authored *Mini-Lessons for Literature Circles* (2004) as both books go into more detail regarding roles and procedures used to embed these within your classroom.

When considering themes you may want to use to normalize talking and learning about traumatic experiences, you may want to create a literature circle unit centered on genocide based on ethnicity. Teachers could provide ample options for students to choose—such as *Night* by Elie Wiesel, *Between Shades of Gray* by Ruta Sepetys, *Refugee* by Alan Gratz, *Internment* by Samira Ahmed, or the many other well-written novels and primary sources that share the perspectives of characters living in war-torn countries or the aftermath and the journey to seek safety and asylum in a new country. Together, students can confront and grapple with the unimaginable human suffering of genocide and analyze not only the reasoning or conflict that led to each but also humanity's resilience to survive and the bravery to bear critical witness to these stories of others. As a class, the groups can return to the whole group and share connections between the characters, settings, actions, and events, creating an opportunity to collaboratively dig deeper into the experiences the characters faced—and also possibly connecting to students' lived experiences.

Katie McGee, a literacy coach and curriculum writer at a district in south Dallas, Texas, gives us an example of how she worked with 8th-grade teachers to create a literature circle text set for the district-required text *To Kill a Mockingbird* by Harper Lee.

> When sitting down to update the upcoming unit for our 8th-grade teachers using *To Kill a Mockingbird* in the Fall of 2018, I felt a sense of dread as local and national news covered the brutal murder of Botham Jean, who was killed in his downtown Dallas apartment by off-duty police officer Amber Guyger. Not only did I live in the same apartment complex that was now covered in news vans and nightly protests, but this was another horrifying example of the ways our justice system and media steal the lives and dignity of Black and Brown Americans. Amid this wave of news, I was grappling with how to make this outdated, in my opinion, arguably problematic, but district-required text relevant for classrooms that were almost filled with Black and Brown students.
>
> I also wanted to honor the fact that the themes and topics of *To Kill a Mockingbird* were possibly triggering for students who were old enough to remember other brutal, highly publicized murders of Black men and women, like Tamir Rice and Trayvon Martin, and subsequent trials of the men and women who killed them. The question became: How can we promote students to explore on their own, in their preferred way, the themes of justice and systemic racism outside of this novel?
>
> We agreed on the overarching theme of justice for the unit. We wanted students to explore how the American justice system has historically treated the accused or victim based on race. To do this, we created a text set from which students would choose multiple texts for literature circles and prepare them for the two Socratic seminars anchoring the unit. To

make this approach cohesive, we brainstormed and chose essential questions that students would use to explore their selected texts. Our essential questions were:

- What does it mean to have "justice"?
- How can works of literature teach us about justice and courage?
- How does historical fiction incorporate real ideas?
- What does it mean to have a jury of your peers?
- What does it mean to be innocent until proven guilty?
- How can people (individuals and/or groups) work toward a more just society?

With our unit theme and essential questions in mind, we left the PLC with homework: We each collected three 8th-grade appropriate texts that could address the essential questions from diverse perspectives. We met the next week to collaboratively choose a set of 5 or 6 texts. After a lively, animated debate, we settled on the following texts:

- Monster, *by Walter Dean Myers*
- The Hate U Give, *by Angie Thomas*
- How It Went Down, *by Kekla Magoon*
- Getting Away With Murder: The True Story of the Emmett Till Case, *by Chris Crowe*
- *"The New Jim Crow," Chapter 5 of* The New Jim Crow, *by Michelle Alexander*
- Collections of articles about Emmett Till, Trayvon Martin, and the Central Park Five from Newsela

Our decisions were not easy, but we knew we needed to explore the justice system for Black Americans from both the side of the victim and the accused, mostly BIPOC authors, and we preferred to have multiple genres so students could choose one fiction text and one nonfiction. After this determination was made, I read each book carefully before creating "book tasting" menus that students could use to decide which texts they wanted to engage with and give to parents and guardians who would be interested in their students' chosen texts.

By engaging with *To Kill a Mockingbird*, the texts, and essential questions through literature circles and the rest of the unit, Katie and her teachers created a goal to give students a chance to shape their own informed opinions and inspire their hopes for the future. The texts allowed students (and teachers) to process what was happening in the world around them through literature and discussion while forming ideas about how they could take action to seek a more just world.

Let's examine how Dr. Lesley Roessing incorporates book clubs, similar to literature circles, when she visits schools and classrooms. Lesley explores why 9/11, the traumatic event all Americans faced in 2001, is an important topic and how it works in a book club format. More information can be found in her 2019 book, *Talking Texts: A Teacher's Guide to Book Clubs across the Curriculum*.

> No historical event may be as unique and complicated to discuss and teach as the events of September 11, 2001, the day terrorists crashed planes into and destroyed the Twin Towers of the World Trade Center. The devastation and impact of these events on our past, present, and future, and as ingrained a part of history as these events are, need to be discussed and understood as much as possible.
>
> At the time of this event, no child in our present K–12 educational system was yet born, so I wasn't as concerned about this study having direct traumatic effects. However, the parents of these readers would have been old enough to have some knowledge of, and even personal experience with, these events, and many families may still be feeling traumatic effects, especially those with family members who died or are just now experiencing consequences to their health.
>
> I have found the most effective way to confront complex topics while presenting various perspectives and differentiated reading experiences for our diverse readers is through book clubs. When classes read five or six novels about 9/11 in small groups of students, they can access differing perspectives of a story and generate essential conversations within each book club and between book clubs. As this chapter has already shared, book clubs give readers safe spaces to discuss sensitive topics and feelings. They generate deeper conversations than when talking as a class or reading individually. The book club meeting format mainly allows for and supports individual interpretations and connections with the stories being read. Book clubs are an effective way to facilitate discussions about trauma and mental health issues.
>
> When I visited schools to facilitate book club reading of novels about 9/11, I generally chose and supplied the novels to be read. First, I selected novels that powerfully relate the story and events but do not present vivid details, such as people jumping out windows to their deaths. Of the twenty-five Middle-Grade and Young Adult novels I have read, there really are only four that I assess as presenting details that I perceive as "graphic" (ironically, two are graphic novels). I also based my choices on matching the readers' age with the protagonists' approximate age. In other words, if I am reading with a 5th-grade class, I suggest novels

> in which the characters are between ages 9 and 13, such as *Eleven; Towers Falling; Nine, Ten: A September 11 Story; I Survived the Attacks of September 11, 2001* (available in prose and graphic versions), and for more proficient readers, *Just a Drop of Water*. For high school classes, I would choose five or six novels that each present a diverse perspective; novels with past and present timelines; novels that take place at Ground Zero and in the Middle East; and novels that are based on present-day effects of 9/11. Reading in book clubs allows readers to choose the novel in which they are the most interested and with which they are most comfortable.

A book pass is a great way to identify which books students will read. As Debbie shared in her example, teachers can also choose certain sections of the book to "book talk" or provide a book tasting.

CONCLUSION

As we have discussed, student engagement and motivation improve when their experiences and identities are valued and intertwined with the curriculum (Gay, 2018; Moll et al., 1992; Nieto & Bode, 2018). How we choose books and which novels we use in our classroom can thus support or impede students' ability to explore their identities. This is important because to build resilience, students need to recognize their strengths, believe in themselves, or develop a high sense of self-efficacy to continue through obstacles or learning challenges (Fisher et al., 2020). They must have opportunities to be agentic—starting with having a choice in what they read. Students must understand their emotions and reactions while recognizing and understanding others' actions and perspectives. Literature allows students to explore how a character problem-solves and makes decisions, which can help them think critically through their situations and determine when to seek additional support and resources.

Suppose we create classrooms that promote "interpersonal practices such as listening, particularly to those different from ourselves, to improve trust, develop community, build empathy, and foster equity" (Andolina & Conklin, 2020, p. 1207). In that case, we increase the number of protective factors in our classrooms, such as cooperation with peers, showing empathy, being assertive, and feeling connected as a community (Holmes et al., 2018).

CHAPTER 4

Critical Dialogue and Discussion in TSLI

For some students, school is not just a place for learning—it's a refuge. Kam *(pseudonym)* came to me on a Monday morning, flustered and panting heavily . . . "Ms. Simmons, I need to talk to you." The tone in his voice alerted me that something was wrong; his usual cheerful voice was dark. Kam felt scared. At just 12 years old, he was experiencing a severe emotional response due to a trigger of the traumas in his life, which was too much for him to handle.

His father was arrested the previous night. His only guardian. His mom was arrested three years prior, serving a life sentence. I knew that his emotional needs were more important than our class work for the day. In my 7th-grade classroom, my number one goal is to create a safe space for my students. Yes, standards and academic instruction are important, but what's the point if students are not mentally present?

"They took my dad, man . . . they took him . . . Ms. S . . . he ain't even do NOTHING." In the span of 10 minutes, Kam yelled, screamed, and cried. I scrapped my agenda for the day, and in class, we talked. I called it Mindful Monday, which continued for the remainder of the year. During this time, my students and I sat in a circle and shared what was going on in our lives, no matter the context or situation. It was a safe space for students to feel heard, seen, and cared for.

I calmed Kam down as much as possible; he didn't feel comfortable leaving my classroom to talk with someone else. I started class by checking in with my students and how they were feeling, with several students sharing how they were tired, sad, frustrated, and a few happy. Inviting them to elaborate, my kids began to open up and share their true feelings. I responded simply with nothing but "Why?" and Kam went first . . . All twenty-one students in my homeroom class were attentive, listening to their peers, sharing connections and sympathy for one another. Even my students who may or may not have had similarly traumatic experiences were open to sharing emotional responses. There was not a dry eye in the room.

Trauma-sensitive discussion can stem from literature, but it can also stem from the needs of our students. At that moment, Kam didn't need to discuss the theme of the short story "Rikki Tikki Tavi." He needed to feel safe, loved, and heard. As educators, we must understand that trauma outside of school affects children in a way that takes over their brains; they are little humans with big feelings. Some of us may never be able to relate to our students' trauma, but trauma-sensitive classrooms and discussions make a world of difference for students and their learning.

—Taylor Simmons, 7th-grade English Language Arts

When we reflect on our pillars shared in Chapter 2, we envision safe and welcoming classrooms facilitated by caring teachers who want students to get to know them and each other. And we think about how dialogue builds and connects relationships, such as with Taylor's opening vignette. Taylor encouraged, promoted, and offered space for her students to share their feelings, creating a trauma-sensitive classroom that supports literacy. Literature provides another avenue to forge a trauma-sensitive literacy classroom (Fisher et al., 2020). Chapter 3 explored *how* and *why* we need a wide array of texts—both canonical and more contemporary literature—and topics embedded within our ELA lessons and instruction. A major takeaway was that all students and their stories matter, meaning we must be willing to use canonical texts *and* more contemporary literature. In this chapter, we explore how our classrooms need to provide students with opportunities to connect, tell their stories, ask others to listen, and potentially offer suggestions.

DIALOGIC TEACHING AND CRITICAL LITERACY PRACTICES

ELA teachers can encourage meaningful and critical thinking, speaking, and listening through relevant discussions about students' interests and experiences. Our classrooms can be liberating spaces that allow students to ask questions, make decisions, and become aware of themselves and their ability to heal with others (Fisher et al., 2020). We are confident that all of you reading this right now already know how crucial and potentially challenging it is to embed critical discussion in your classrooms.

And when we say critical, we mean beyond the initiate-respond-evaluate structure often seen in classrooms where a teacher is expecting a specific response, someone responds (usually with a one- or two-word answer), and the teacher evaluates the response (Cazden, 1988). When we use the term "critical dialogue," we refer to an active and ongoing dialogue that students have with a text, the author, the time period of the writing, and one another. With this type of analysis, teachers no longer ask if students "get it"; they ask what their students are taking away from the text and instruction as it relates to them and their lives—how it *matters* to the students (Winn et al., 2021).

When we consider what this looks like in our classrooms, dialogic ELA teaching requires instruction to be viewed as organic—making room for dialogue that leads to co-constructed interpretations with one another and between readers (Rosenblatt, 1994. It cannot stem from a scripted and preplanned lesson. Antoinetta J. Rogers, a secondary ELA teacher colleague, shared her thoughts about education with Rachelle during one of their class sessions: "Education is an organic entity. How we teach and deliver lessons to students does not originate from concrete strategies but organic vessels that should be tailored to meet the individual needs of each student." Dialogic teaching is one way to align with Mrs. Rogers's mindset as it responds to students' questions or thoughts shared during reading, with teachers asking students to elaborate on their opinions to support a collective interpretation and meaning (Rigell & Banack, 2021).

By engaging in this dialogue, students connect what they already know with what they did not know and expand their understanding of themselves, others, the world, and significant cultural and societal issues (Fisher et al., 2020; Piazza et al., 2015). When speaking specifically about literature, reading literature is a dialogic, interpretive process (Bakhtin, 1984), meaning there isn't one set interpretation. As shared in Chapter 3, this means that our students read about situations, events, and characters they can relate to—mirrors—*and* read about experiences that they cannot relate to—windows. This expansive reading allows students to connect and learn about others, which is essential because all experiences are different.

Additionally, this type of reading and learning with others prompts students to evaluate preconceived notions and beliefs critically. More importantly, students assess potential biases of what they are reading—from the standpoint of the content and related to the author. For instance, students may question the author's motive in writing the text, evaluate if character portrayals are accurate and authentic, and even investigate if the author is an expert in the content or topic. In other words, the students question the story's authenticity and the voices shared through the characters and plot (Donovan & Toliver, 2019). Students must closely read the words on the page, between the lines, interpret personal assumptions, and research to understand potential misrepresentation or inaccurate portrayals.

As ELA teachers, we want our students to examine, analyze, and challenge the messages shared critically and not shared by authors to better understand differing experiences, cultures, and lives. We want students to determine the plot, central idea, and other story elements. We also want students to examine power relations to "dismantle inequitable ways of being" (Vasquez et al., 2019, p. 301) and to grapple with why there are certain political and social groups that have more access to power and wealth than others (Bishop, 2014). Students must question what is "truth," which positions readers to question the author's intent and trustworthiness (Applebee & Langer, 2013; Janks, 2005). Students must be active, often promoting agency as they solve and challenge current issues of an unjust world (Bishop, 2014; Janks, 2010; Luke, 2012) and learn about the resiliency of those experiencing trauma and the hardships they face (Fisher et al., 2020). In other words, when we ask students to be critical readers and analyzers, we can create opportunities for students to heal, have a voice, become agentic and empowered, and understand the traumatic experiences many students, including themselves, face (Dutro, 2019; Fisher et al., 2020). To learn more about critical literacy and culturally sustaining literacy instruction, check out the following titles:

- *Acts of Resistance: Subversive Teaching in the English Language Arts Classroom* edited by J. Dyches, B. Sams, and A. S. Boyd.
- *Connecting Theory and Practice in Middle School Literacy: Critical Conversations* edited by J. DeHart, C. Meyer, and K. Walker.
- *Cultivating Genius: An Equity Framework for Culturally and Historically Responsive Literacy* by G. E. Muhammad.
- *Culturally Responsive Teaching: Theory, Research, and Practice* by G. Gay.
- *Culturally Sustaining Literacy Pedagogies: Honoring Students' Heritages, Literacies, and Languages* edited by S. Chambers Cantrell, D. Walker-Dalhouse, and A. M. Lazar.
- *Culturally Sustaining Pedagogies: Teaching and Learning for Justice in a Changing World* edited by D. Paris and H. S. Alim.
- *Educating for empathy: Literacy learning and civic engagement* by N. Mirra.
- *It's Not "One More Thing": Culturally Responsive and Affirming Strategies in K–12 Literacy Classrooms* by A. Swenson Ticknor, C. Howard, and M. Overstreet.
- *Literacy is Liberation: Working toward Justice through Culturally Relevant Teaching* by K. N. Parker.
- *Race, Justice, and Activism in Literacy Instruction* by V. Kinloch, T. Burkhard, and C. Penn.
- *Teaching the "Taboo": Diverse and Inclusive Literature Is the Way* edited by R. S. Savitz, L. D., Roberts, and J. DeHart.

Reciprocal Process of Critical Testimony and Bearing Witness

In 2019, Elizabeth Dutro published her book *The Vulnerable Heart of Literacy: Centering Trauma as a Powerful Pedagogy*, where she reminds educators of the powerful act and reciprocal process of sharing testimony and bearing critical witness as a way to communicate and learn with and from our students. This robust dialogue has been around for years as people share stories with friends and others either to gather feedback or to have someone listen. This process works just as well in our classrooms. As trauma-sensitive literacy educators, we create classrooms where students first think and reflect on who they are, their lived experiences and beliefs, and their feelings.

According to Dutro (2019), testimony is the act of "attesting to an experience," while witnessing is listening to another's testimony of their own experience. However, witnessing can be much more, even leading others to advocate for "students and work toward social justice" (p. 24). This reciprocal process invites students to share their experiences and perspectives through dialogic discussion (Rigell & Banack, 2021), where students can then ask questions that provoke additional discussion (Winn et al., 2021). Witnessing can also support healing (Fisher et al., 2020).

For example, when I (Rachelle) recently taught a cultural diversity course for teachers seeking a master's in education, I started the first lesson by stating that I am still learning. I wanted teachers to understand that we will have many questions as we learn about diversity, culture, racism, and oppression, and how society has promoted some and harmed others. As we grapple with what we always define as "truth," we must understand that we may feel uncomfortable, but we must learn and grow as educators and, ultimately, as humans. At the end of the semester, the teachers shared that they were more comfortable being vulnerable because I was vulnerable when I shared stories of learning about race and mistakes made throughout my years of teaching.

Here is another example of how I shared my vulnerability with students when reading *I Must Betray You* by Ruta Sepetys. This book tells the story of 17-year-old Cristian, who lived in Romania in 1989 when it was under Communist control. The story shares how children were blackmailed and harassed to monitor, spy on, and report friends and neighbors who weren't following the rules of Ceausescu, a Romanian communist dictator. Cristian and the other characters lived in constant fear. Provided only the bare minimum to survive, they stood in line all day for meager food portions insufficient to feed the entire family—if they received any. This part of the novel is where I share with students my familial connections to Romania and how my grandmother was from there before living as a Jew in a concentration camp during the Holocaust.

As we read, we briefly discuss the treatment of Jews years before; I share stories my mother and grandparents told me. We talk about how my grandparents' neighbors and friends turned on them and other Jews in Poland and Romania. We also talk about how many of my mother's family did not survive the Holocaust; we discuss how even though she was born after WWII, she was born in a deportation camp and lived there for three years in deplorable conditions. This is an example of what Dutro (2019) calls giving testimony because I shared examples of my family's trauma in personal connections to the text. I must share my connections to trauma because—as Dutro points out—in critical witness and testimony, students must understand that everyone can experience trauma. This is not a situation where teachers are the healers and students are the only ones needing healing.

And while I make it clear that no story like mine or that of Cristian's is the same for others, while we read and I share, I invite students to share their connections and ask their questions. Often, students ask questions for which I do not have immediate answers—which is okay. My students learn early on that I do not know everything. I make it clear from the start that I am still learning—and that I research and learn by listening to others' experiences and thoughts.

Lysaker and colleagues (2011) explain that when teachers demonstrate authentic responses to a text as they read, as in the previous example, and invite students to make similar personal connections between the text and the reader's lived experiences, students' reading comprehension is supported. Students also develop empathy for others, moving from accepting differences to valuing and appreciating diversity. When students engage in the latter, they learn content presented in the class and learn to explore and interpret the world and others (Freire, 1970).

Thus, learning from students and providing space for students to share their connections and stories is necessary for a trauma-sensitive literacy classroom. Often, students witness how "characters must adapt and adopt new modes of learning and communication even through challenges, hardship, and turmoil, which call for persistence, resilience, and self-affirmation" (Rodríguez, 2019, p. xvi). In trauma-sensitive literacy classrooms, students connect with these characters and experiences, learn from them, and feel heard and seen. They develop hope and healing for themselves as they grapple with the characters' experiences, connect with their situations, and develop empathy for others in similar circumstances (Fisher et al., 2020). These moments are powerful for classmates and us to listen to and learn from, bearing critical witness to someone we know and the problems and issues they face. Often, we want to jump in as educators to connect with our students and their experiences—building the strong relationship discussed in Chapter 2 and demonstrating to our students that we will address their concerns and issues when they arise.

However, we must also understand that not all books provide a way for us to share a testimony with our students—because some books will not be mirrors. We may relate on the surface or to certain events in a novel but not to the central conflict or the protagonist. In these cases, it is vital to be honest when we read these stories and invite students to connect even when we cannot. Importantly, we must understand that students are taking a leap of faith by sharing, as they do not have a guarantee that their testimony will be received with compassion, respect, and empathy. This leap of faith is precisely what Jennifer Morrison's student, Tanya, had to take. Let's step into Jennifer's classroom to read about a powerful dialogic experience.

One of my favorite pieces of literature is Tennessee Williams's (1947) *A Streetcar Named Desire*, and I was fortunate enough to teach it for several years with 11th-grade students. Of course, I was drawn to Williams's poetic writing and ability to generate rich, steamy, sultry images of New Orleans, which seemed so exotic and intriguing to my perceptions. Even from my first reading of the play, I was fascinated by the dynamic tensions between its three primary characters—Stanley, Stella, and Blanche—and the verbal and physical dances they performed as they interacted. To me, the play was a study of people and how they operate in harmony or conflict with one another, their pasts, and their environments. In my second year of teaching the play, I realized *Streetcar* is a play about power—the attempt for characters to maintain power, to use their social or past positions to gain power, to exert physical or psychological force to win power, to use language to position others in subversive positions, to manipulate third parties as ransom in power negotiations. It is about how we dominate others by bending their wills to ours and how we yield our power, handing it up without question to our oppressors. It is about the fragility of our positions and identities, however tenuous or fallacious, that we generate to survive in uncertain social and cultural situations.

This is the lens through which I taught the play within a thematic unit of "Influences on the Individual." At first, I did not realize the impact such a literary framing would have on the dialogue that would subsequently emerge within my classroom. I began by discussing the concept of power with my students—examining societal, institutionalized, personal, and political perspectives and understanding how power could "influence individuals."

As we read, enacted, and discussed the play's first scenes, we returned to how power dynamics were emerging. When we arrived at the scene where Stanley hits his wife Stella, one of my students, a 16-year-old girl named Tanya (pseudonym), spoke out vigorously and passionately. She openly shared that she was in a physically abusive relationship with her older boyfriend. As she interpreted the power Stanley exerts on Stella when he strikes her, Tanya argued the motivation behind his actions—power over his wife in a situation that threatened his dominant position over her: a need to demonstrate his ability as a feral male to control "his woman" in front of his friends. Her words tumbled from her, one idea frantically building on the next as she wove a personal tapestry through her response to the literary text. Her dialogue moved from a description of her present abuse to a realization of how the power dynamics in the play paralleled the actions of her boyfriend and herself. The play represented Tanya's lived experience, and by reading about it from a more objective position, she could see how power and control played

> out in her own life. Her revelation within her circumstances became my revelation of the play's commentary on how power permeates our everyday actions and interactions.
>
> Using literacy vehicles such as *A Streetcar Named Desire*, which so clearly demonstrates the push and pull, oppression, and subjugation of individuals embedded within power structures, helps students to unpack and discuss lived experiences through a screen that can be as protective as they need it to be. Establishing a framework that addressed power within a literary text allowed interrelational dynamics within my classroom and can help students like Tanya make their own experiences of domination visible and illuminate the more subtle institutionalized forms of repression that occur within a complex, multifaceted society.

What Dr. Morrison experienced in her classroom with her students is an excellent example of how students will engage with what they are reading, connect with a character or action, and share their testimony with others. Tanya's empowerment to speak up and realize her abusive situation prompted Dr. Morrison, who bore witness, to realize the necessity for creating space for these dialogic experiences.

Reading Conferences

While we can create spaces and opportunities for our students to share and connect as an entire class, with many of these spaces aligning with Benard's four main traits of resilient students discussed in Chapter 1, we can also provide individual time to get to know our students in this way. Reading conferences are relatively common in elementary classrooms and are gaining traction in middle and high school settings. Reading conferences happen in a one-on-one setting with a student, allowing them to discuss what they are reading, share "aha" moments, connect to whole-group lessons, and demonstrate learning or skill development—while teachers can scaffold instruction, chat about data, set student-created accountability goals based on their specific needs and interests, and most importantly, relay personal information about things that impact students' lives and studies (Serafini, 2001; Taylor, 2020).

Reading conferences are often a lifeline for many students who have built trust and rapport with the teacher but are not yet comfortable speaking in front of the class. This is why Atwell (2015) used the metaphor of a dining room table to describe reading conferences—they create space for easy connections and sharing. This time together is also a valuable step in building relationships with students.

While this is hypothetical, I (Rachelle) share an example of a reading conference that is representative of the years of reading conferences conducted with students. Each day, during our 90-minute reading/ELA block, my students either met with me in conferences or in small-group instruction while other students worked in their small groups. When Kelly came up to our conference table, she brought her book and journal, where she kept her questions and connections between her independent reading novel and herself. After reviewing my notes from the previous reading conference with Kelly the week before, I knew she was working on analyzing character development in her novel, as this was something she needed to practice. However, that was not the case. While she did provide a recap of what she had read in the past week, she quickly mentioned her connection with the protagonist. I had read this book, so I knew the main character was pregnant and trying to decide what she wanted to know, exploring options.

Therefore, instead of discussing how the main character developed and connected with other characters, I stopped and asked Kelly if she was okay, and if she wanted to talk with me more about this topic or if she wanted to see the school counselor. Asking these questions first allowed her to decide if she wanted to continue this conversation or if she needed more time and space. She quickly informed me how she brought it up to me because I was the adult in her life that she felt safest talking to and that she worried about telling her mother just yet.

Over the next 20 minutes, we discussed why she worried about talking with her mother and identified a few potential next steps. We took time to investigate resources for each option she wanted to explore, and we discussed setting up an appointment with the local Planned Parenthood. Because she was 18, she had some leeway about whom she told and when. Additionally, with her approval, I called our school counselor, whom I had already extensively worked with and trusted to appropriately and sensitively talk with Kelly. Near the end of our conference, our school counselor came and met with my student, leading to additional conversations during lunch and over the next few days. At times, the student requested that I be present during these meetings, but she slowly started to trust the school counselor as much as I did and met with her one-on-one after the first week.

Reading conferences were one way I built relationships with my students as I focused on the standards and reteaching lessons, but I also let my students use the space to talk through their feelings and situations, even if not directly connected with a text. As noted in my example, I prioritized holding weekly conferences so I could continue working with individual students based on their needs.

Traditionally, reading conferences have a reasonably predictable structure, such as starting with a recap of previous discussions, opening the discussion up by asking the student what they want to share, and ending with the student creating some goals for the next meeting (Atwell, 2015; Serafini, 2001). Students can create goals related to specific comprehension strategies taught during whole group, such as annotating text, or their goal could be to read a certain number of pages in their independent choice book. These one-on-one times allow us to understand that a student is disengaging. Tovani (2021) brilliantly describes students' seeming disengagement in terms of masks. She notes that students may wear the mask of the class clown, the mask of minimal effort, the mask of anger and apathy, and many others. Because students often wear these masks, we must figure out how we can support our students to connect with us, each other, and the texts we read in our classrooms. Conferences provide an avenue to help students construct meaning, practice reading, and engage personally and culturally with reading at their pace and based on their questions (Serravallo & Goldberg, 2007).

Anticipation Guide

There are also some specific activities that we can use in our classrooms to structure critical dialogue. One of our favorites is the Anticipation Guide. Anticipation Guides engage students in thinking about specific concepts and statements before reading a text or novel. A prereading activity prompts students to explore their attitudes and beliefs about the text topic and listen to others' perspectives and opinions. It is also a great way to support students to reflect on how their beliefs may shift as they read and discuss ideas (Fisher et al., 2020).

To create an Anticipation Guide, teachers write three to five statements that offer multiple perspectives, interpretations, or beliefs and then ask students to decide if they "agree" or "disagree" or to choose "true" or "false" for each statement. These statements can be read to the entire class with time for students to react, discuss, and even move around the room to represent their choice (think four-corner activities). Alternatively, students can read through all statements and make decisions. Then teachers can ask student volunteers to share their reasoning for each question's choice.

One benefit of Anticipation Guides is that they activate students' background knowledge *and* pique their curiosity about what they will read and learn about in the upcoming text or unit. Anticipation Guides can be structured with isolated ideas and mainly connected to the topic, or the questions can be a series of statements. Through conversation with one another and the whole class, the teacher can gauge students' interest and determine potential supplemental and background information needed before starting the planned upcoming lessons. Additionally, Anticipation Guides can support students in making predictions about what they will read and setting a purpose for the upcoming unit or lesson.

As with all new activities and strategies, it is crucial to model how to personally consider and reflect on each statement and then share reasoning. We suggest taking the first question together, reading it aloud, and modeling how to think through what the question asks, how it relates to personal experiences and beliefs, and how to use that information to make decisions. Teachers can then invite students to engage with the same question, asking them if they agree or disagree or if it is true or false, prompting them to consider why. The discussion piece is crucial for helping students understand student perspectives and learn from one another's lived experiences. It can also support teachers in determining the next steps for introducing the unit or text. Therefore, these questions or statements should not have a "right" answer because the goal is to get students thinking and sharing. Finally, the Anticipation Guide can be an after-reading activity where students can check their predictions and possibly change their initial opinions.

Let's step into Rachel Long's high school ELA classroom and learn why and how she uses an Anticipation Guide to support her students' discussion of complex topics.

> One of the first things we learn as preservice educators is to build and sustain relationships with our students. Relationships are essential in education. My students thrive in an environment where they feel connected to and trust their teachers. Therefore, creating a safe and welcoming community is crucial for me and my classroom because that is where most learning occurs. As easy as it is to tell incoming teachers to start with building relationships, this is not always the most straightforward task when we have five full classes of students with a variety of needs.
>
> Some of the simplest exercises give our class the most rewarding outcome and provide space for students to share their thoughts and experiences. For example, I started my unit on *Macbeth* with a simple Anticipation Guide. I love Anticipation Guides because they spark meaningful discussions that relate the content to modern life and give students an idea about the literature and why its underlying themes can be relevant. Using Anticipation Guides can be done in several ways to get students engaged. First, a teacher must create or find a list of statements directly related to the piece of literature. I try to use meaningful, engaging, and accessible statements for students to explore on a deeper level. Below is a list of statements used with my students:
>
> 1. Behind every great man is a great woman.
> 2. Witches, demons, and ghosts exist.
> 3. Sometimes, it is necessary to do something wrong to get what you want.
> 4. Traitors should be executed.
> 5. Success is worth any price you have to pay.
> 6. You should never compromise your values.
> 7. The direction of our lives is decided by something or someone else (fate), not by our actions.

8. Being powerful usually is the same thing as being happy.
9. Everyone is capable of murder under the right circumstances.
10. One mistake often leads to another.

Initially, these questions were provided to students to consider and write about independently. However, they weren't feeling it, and neither was I. The students expressed that they wanted to just talk about each one. Students gave profound, well-thought-out answers to every statement. One of the longest conversations stemmed from the statement, "we should be careful whom we trust" and "everyone is capable of murder under the right circumstances." First, they discussed backstabbing friends or cheating boyfriends/girlfriends. Then, a student openly discussed her time living in a group home. She told us about the people in charge and some of the restrictions she faces because of her diagnosis. Listening, or bearing witness, was difficult for students, but even as a new transfer student, she felt safe and trusted her classmates and me enough to share these intimate details of her life. Preparing classes for things like this is challenging because it was unplanned. However, our use of critical discussion year-round created a habit of being open and honest with each other. It also helped that this was a smaller group. Sometimes, teachers just need to allow students to connect on a routine basis because their experiences shape who they are and help them learn and grow.

When discussing the statement, "everyone is capable of murder under the right circumstances," most students wanted to openly discuss this, as we had lost three students over the past year to gun violence. Some students were okay with discussing this topic. For students who were silent or not ready to speak, I simply told the class we would handle this with care and be open and respectful to one another, but we would not force anyone to talk if they didn't want to. Students also always have the option to grab my guidance pass and leave quietly when needed. I asked students to keep an open mind, respect each other's opinions, and allow everyone to share. One student said he thought he could be capable of murder if someone ever hurt his younger sibling. Another student said she related to this because she had younger cousins and siblings. This is tough to hear as a teacher but very real for these students. If teachers hear something like this, I suggest that teachers give students space to share. However, in these situations, I pull the student for an individual chat after class to check in and remind them that teachers are mandated reporters who must share these scenarios with their guidance counselor, for example.

Later that evening, I spoke with a student from the class who expressed his interest in getting a care package together for her. Coincidentally, this

> student lives next door to me, so his mother reached out and came to me in tears. She said he talked with her and told her he had no idea people lived like this. The importance of having these guided discussions with students is significant in this scenario because so many students were able to be empathetic with their classmates.

As Rachel shared, she was able to get to know her students and build strong relationships through these conversations. Because of how she set up her classroom and provided background, she created a safe space for her students to share and connect with their peers. By doing so, her students knew they were welcome to share their experiences and ask their questions, setting the tone that all occasions were part of her classroom instruction, materials, and discussion—even if it meant changing her plans at a moment's notice.

Circle of Viewpoints

Another great critical dialogue strategy is Circle of Viewpoints. Fisher and colleagues (2020) shared how Circle of Viewpoints is a trauma-sensitive practice that allows students to discuss as they read—stopping and debriefing what they are learning about the characters and their interpretations. Conversations can relate to the dynamic characters presented, their backgrounds provided through flashbacks, and their actions while enduring the traumatic experience. As the novel evolves, students discuss how significant characters in the book perceive the events taking place and their responses to traumatic experiences. Students can explore how others treat characters and which characters exhibit empathy or resiliency. After completing the novel, students discuss how their thinking has remained the same or changed and why.

This may seem unclear at first, so let's hear how Emma Willard uses this strategy in her 7th-grade ELA and social studies classroom. She provides an example using the novel *Maniac Magee* by Jerry Spinelli.

> To begin, I let students know we will be working on a perspective-taking activity. Our task as readers is to understand the motivations behind character choices in the novel. It's not enough to simply identify the action in the story and call it the plot. We must analyze why these events occur and how they connect each character. Using the circle of viewpoints, we can analyze how a character's background and experiences affect their behavior (and the plot). By exploring the different perspectives that characters can have, students can also better understand the different views of their peers. Suppose we can guide students to look for and identify coping strategies and the motivation behind a character's actions. In that case, they will begin to understand

that everyone is dealing with complex emotions, which may lead to a better understanding of themselves and their peers.

At times, students struggle to get started, so here is an example of thinking questions I share with my students to help them get unstuck:

- Can two people react to the same situation differently?
- How do our actions affect other people?
- In what ways does the past influence our future?
- Does the plot affect the characters, or do the characters affect the plot?

The next step for students is to work in groups to analyze specific events from the novel using the following three questions:

1. I am thinking of [an event, a topic, another character] from the point of view of [the selected character].
2. I think . . . because . . .
3. A question or concern I have from this viewpoint is . . .

For example, each group would analyze the motivations of the main character, Maniac Magee (MM), and how his response to conflict drives the plot. One potential analysis could be when MM runs away from his aunt and uncle's house. Students could analyze the event by trying to understand why MM ran away from home. To determine why MM was compelled to run away, they may use this starting prompt: "I think MM ran away because . . ."

As I move around the room, if I see groups or students struggling, I prompt them with the previously mentioned thinking questions and remind them to use their perspective-taking vocabulary to discuss MM's actions. We teach students about degrees of emotion, proactive vs. reactive response, and coping strategies during our SEL Connect time, which is influenced by resources from *Coping Power, 7 Habits of the Highly Effective Teenager, and How to be a Person*. However, I also reinforce these in my classroom during our mindful moments at the beginning of class.

Here is a sample response using our vocabulary: MM's decision to run away was reactive because he was responding to his negative feelings of loneliness and abandonment. When students move on to their concerns with MM's choice, they should discuss other ways MM could have coped with his situation. For example: if MM had more friends to talk to or activities to take his mind off losing his parents, he might not have run away. Other possible topics could include when MM runs away from the

Beale home, when MM confronts Mars Bar, or when MM invites Mars Bar to the party.

As students move through the circle of viewpoints, it is essential to use guiding questions to help them analyze whether MM's response is proactive or reactive, how his past influences his decisions in the present, and how the plot would change without his previous experiences. As students move on with their questions/concerns, they analyze how he could have coped differently and how his negative coping strategies are affecting him.

After a set amount of time, I bring students back as a group to discuss and share their findings. Using stop-and-jot questions, I ask them if they can relate to any of MM's experiences. Using a watch or timer, I give students 1 to 2 minutes after each question to jot down their answers before talking to their neighbors. When the time is up, I invite the whole group to discuss, or I may have pairs discuss their solutions, but they aren't required to share with the class. The Stop and Jots can serve as progress monitoring for the activity. Here are a few example questions I have used with this novel:

- Would you have behaved the same as Maniac Magee?
- What are some ways that you cope when you're feeling stressed?
- How can you be proactive when faced with difficult situations?
- Is it fair to use our past as an excuse for our current actions?

A potential extension to Circle of Viewpoints is what Eliza Ramirez and Sarah Donovan (2021) describe as Harm and Healing Analysis (see their article "Harm and Healing: Reading with an ABAR [Anti-bias, Antiracist] Lens" for process and example questions). While students read, they identify a harm in the novel that has occurred, as noted by Emma in her snapshot, *and* students explore what was "done or not done to repair the harm" (p. 56). Students learn to examine people, actions, and systems that cause harm and that there isn't one path toward healing, resilience, and joy.

What is important to note from Emma's classroom is that these questions are open-ended, meaning that students will have various interpretations—which is a feature of this instructional activity. As Rosenblatt (1994) shared decades ago, we read and interpret literature based on many factors. Students' lived experiences, cultural and racial identities, places of origin, and many other elements of what makes them who they are may lead them to various interpretations. This does not mean that *all* interpretations of a story or passage are appropriate. What it does mean is that we need to provide space for students to engage in group work, share their thoughts and ideas, and explain how they formed their interpretation—using information and evidence from the text. Winn and her colleagues (2021) mention that reading isn't a "replicable act of decoding and comprehending" that requires a single-story interpretation that must fit within our "preconfigured understanding of a text" (p. 51). Instead, our readers create "divergent and imaginative analyses" that can lead to transformational conversations as a class (Aukerman, 2013; Winn et al., 2021, p. 50).

Therefore, we need to establish a classroom environment where students feel confident, engaged, and safe and where their ability to share understanding and justification for diverse interpretations is appreciated and valued over simply giving a correct response (Corcoran & Mamalakis, 2009; Vlach & Burcie, 2010). When we allow students to share their understanding, which may differ from ours or from the "right" answer we were expecting, we promote the knowledge that it is safe to try new things in our classrooms (i.e., interpreting and expressing reasoning, collaborating in small groups, and becoming active learners setting personal goals). This may mean that while we read a poem and have our interpretation, we want our students to share their thoughts and reasoning. Unique experiences and backgrounds provide new ways to view and understand what we read (Rosenblatt, 1994). At times, the new interpretation will make sense based on the additional information shared by the student. Other times, the interpretation may not work as well as another presented (Kane et al., 2021).

Ultimately, the goal of building a sense of community in a classroom is to understand that I, the teacher, am not the only expert in the room. Students are part of the learning process. Together, they collaborate to make meaning and form interpretations, opening new pathways for understanding, engaging, and developing resilience, creating spaces that "restore, restory, and resist" (Winn et al., 2021). This classroom is not silent, with all students in neat rows, as has been the case in years past. Instead, students are turning to one another, asking questions, sharing in excitement about something they read, and connecting in ways that would not occur in a classroom where the teacher is the primary focus during learning. Students quickly learn to trust that their lives and growth are essential to everyone in the room, which also means that their voices and story matter.

CONCLUSION

Throughout this chapter, we shared how dialogue supports drawing on students' lived experiences in positive, proactive, and protective ways as they explore characters and their own experiences, questions, and realities within instruction. When we tackle complex subjects head on to show our students that they and their hardships are part of the classroom and create space for discussing these experiences, we create TSLI that promotes hope, healing, and learning options. We shared various ways you can embed these necessary practices in your classroom, with a takeaway that each teacher listened closely to their students—because their voices and stories matter most.

At the start of this chapter, we read Antoinetta Rogers's stance on teaching and learning—it is organic. And it *must* be created with our students not only in mind but with their thoughts and needs. However, as Dutro and Caasi (2022) point out, how we draw on students' lived experiences are not as explicitly explained. However, we know our curricula instruction must let our students see themselves, and for students to *be* themselves, as part of "enacting the humanizing ability of literacy" (Nguyen, 2018, p. 17). Ultimately, in a TSLI classroom, we need to let our students' experiences and stories live and breathe within our classroom dialogue and instruction, and we must allow students to connect with us and one another. We must also critically reflect on what we are teaching and how we are teaching it—either in ways that promote student making and sharing connections or ways that leave students feeling traumatized.

CHAPTER 5

Using Writing in TSLI

I (Britnie) have clear memories of my first few years teaching creative writing with 9th-graders. I was proud of the writing instruction I had done and thrilled as I read their work. They were developing a command of imagery; they were using more active verbs; they were borrowing craft techniques from Sandra Cisneros—yes, THE Sandra Cisneros—which I had used as a mentor text. Most importantly, they were developing their sense of voice. I remember smiling at my desk, bowled over: "My God," I thought. "Teaching works."

And then I came to Shaquawn's paper. Shaquawn had trouble managing his anger. He was loud, always yelling. He was often in the principal's office because he'd had another altercation during passing period, sometimes with peers, sometimes with teachers. His command of written language had landed him in my "College Prep A" class, which was code for the lowest tracked ELA class. I remember he also wrote vignettes about his life and his father. They were specific, detailed, full of images and sound. Unlike so much beginning writing, Shaquawn's papers did not give overarching, summative adjectives that mask the experience of a thing and dull away its edges. His papers used active verbs and imagery, as I had taught him, to detail how child abuse looks, how it sounds, how it smells.

As I read Shaquawn's stories, I blinked uncomprehendingly, knowing only that I didn't know what to do. The specificity and detail I had so proudly taught him landed me there, staring at his page, swallowing. How would I write feedback on this? How would I respond to the vulnerability on this page? The next vignette brought me to tears. It described Shaquawn's plans for his own fatherhood. It too was a case study in the use of imagery, full of sights and sounds and smells and plans—so many specific plans. But these were plans of life and love. He would never leave wordlessly in the middle of the night. He would never hit his kids on their birthdays. Or ever. I cried. Uselessly, I thought about juxtaposition. Shaquawn knew how to use juxtaposition—or, more accurately, he probably wasn't aware that he had used juxtaposition, but I could teach him that. I could show him how he had used it and explain how it added to the vast power of his work. I could point out how moving his honesty was and how strong his choice of verbs was. But I didn't know if I should—how could I meet this tragedy with a dry treatise on juxtaposition? It felt wrong, somehow. But then, I didn't know what would be right. I am still unsure if

I do, but this chapter is a step along that path. This chapter suggests that I should have helped Shaquawn to see the power of his use of juxtaposition; I should have pointed out the power of his verbs and his use of sound. I should have told him that I saw the writer in him and the resilience in him because they both glowed—so beautifully—off his pages. I should have told Shaquawn I was so sorry about what happened to him. I should have told Shaquawn I was honored to have been trusted with his story.

A widespread assumption in our culture is that writing is a form of catharsis—that it is, in and of itself, healing. A one-minute Google search leads us to "12 Quotes about Writing in Honor of World Trauma Day" (Smith, 2019) and the "Top 35 Writing and Healing Quotes" (Quotestats.com, 2022). As trauma-sensitive literacy teachers, we must verify this assumption: Can writing support healing? Fortunately, clinical psychologists have studied this question. The answer seems clear and resounding: "Yes." However, for teachers, the answer is a bit more complicated. Let's start by describing what clinical psychologists have found and then explore the implications of their findings for teachers.

Over the last 4 decades, James Pennebaker of the University of Texas at Austin has studied the clinical relationship between expressive writing and mental and physical health. In these studies, participants were invited to a lab and asked to "write continuously about the most upsetting or traumatic experience of [their] entire li[ves]" (Pennebaker & Smyth, 2016, p. 16). Over his long career, Pennebaker and his colleagues have found that even short stints of writing—typically 15 minutes of continuous writing over 4 consecutive days—can improve individuals' physical and mental health:

> [P]eople who wrote about their deepest thoughts and feelings related to stressful or traumatic experiences had reliable improvements in health in the two to three months after writing. Although there were also improvements in people's self-reports of their health, there were equally large effects on people's physiological functioning. (Pennebaker and Smyth, 2016, p. 21)

For example, one study found that, in clinical settings, individuals who participated in the expressive writing intervention went to the doctor less frequently over the next 6 months than their peers who wrote about issues unrelated to their life experiences or trauma. Those who wrote about their experiences showed enhanced immune function 6 weeks after the intervention and reported an improved overall sense of well-being and purpose (Pennebaker & Smyth, 2016).

Since Pennebaker's landmark work was first published in 1986, over 200 clinical studies have found that expressive writing can reduce stress, anxiety, and even depression; enhance the quality of sleep and performance; and support improved focus and clarity (Siegel-Acevado, 2021). Glass and colleagues (2019), for example, studied a 6-week writing intervention, which included "expressive, transactional, poetic, affirmative, legacy, and mindful writing prompts." They found that writing "increases resilience, and decreases depressive symptoms, perceived stress, and rumination in an outpatient sample of those reporting trauma in the past year" (p. 240).

Thus, the clinical research community seems to agree that expressive writing can "be considered an evidence-based treatment for posttraumatic stress and constitutes a useful treatment alternative for patients who do not respond to other evidence-based therapies" (Mirgain & Singles, 2016, p. 2). Clinical psychologists are finding—on a larger scale—what Anne Frank observed so many years ago: "I can shake off everything as I write: My sorrows disappear, courage is reborn."

WHAT ABOUT TEACHERS? SHOULD WE BE USING EXPRESSIVE WRITING TO SUPPORT STUDENTS EXPERIENCING TRAUMA?

Given these promising findings, should we, as teachers, jump right in and start asking students to write about their experiences of trauma? As we know, teachers are not trained psychologists or therapists, and we should not act in the classroom as though we are. Also, these expressive writing interventions were typically completed in a lab setting, which is very different from middle and high school classrooms, which are often replete with social consequences, anxieties, and traumas. Thus, we must consider the pedagogical implications of asking students to write about their traumas.

Research began looking into relationships among trauma, emotion, and writing pedagogies, particularly in higher education, in the 1970s. By the late 1980s and early 1990s, buoyed by findings by Pennebaker and others, instructors of writing began to adopt counseling-based approaches in the writing classroom (Day, 2019). Many professors were excited by psychologists' findings about relationships between writing and catharsis because these findings appeared to confirm what many writers had experienced themselves: that the work of writing can be healing. Author Jeanette Winterson, who penned the hilarious and poignant memoir *Oranges Are Not the Only Fruit*, put it this way: "Creativity is on the side of health—it isn't the thing that drives us mad; it is the capacity in us that tries to save us from madness" (Smith, 2019, n.p.). Indeed, advocates of this line of thinking often argue that writing instructors should hold themselves ethically responsible for leveraging writing's potential healing properties (Day, 2019).

However, some researchers and theorists on writing saw problems with this approach: They noted that writing instructors are not trained for therapy and should not meddle in such serious business. Others have worried that bringing trauma into the classroom might—at worst—retraumatize students while—at best—creating ethical dilemmas in grading. Still, others have argued that bringing trauma into the classroom might "encourage navel gazing and individualism, at the expense of intellectual development" (Day, 2019, p. 207). In short, there was a concern that teachers might unknowingly shift away from academics and into the realm of guidance counseling.

Perhaps, the words above might have echoed some of your concerns about trauma and writing instruction. If that's the case, we applaud you. As responsible educators, we should be asking these questions. Unfortunately, they do not have easy answers. In the following sections, we will discuss what pedagogical research has to say about many of these issues. Our overarching stance on bringing trauma into writing instruction is this: We hope you are excited by the possibilities for healing that writing can present. We also hope you are forthright and sober about the role you can—and should—take up concerning trauma and writing instruction. If you feel that inviting trauma into your classroom is risky, you should know that you are right. However, we also insist that leaving trauma out of writing is risky as well—from a pedagogical standpoint and from the perspective of caring for our students (Day, 2019; Dutro, 2019; Fisher et al., 2020).

As we described in Chapters 1 and 2, research on trauma has long recognized that those who experience it are often predisposed to feel shame and secretiveness around their experiences of trauma, but secretiveness can itself lead to health problems and increased feelings of shame and anxiety (Fisher et al., 2020; Pennebaker & Smyth, 2016). Indeed, the perceived inability to share what has happened often compounds trauma's adverse physical and mental effects. Thus, we should listen to clinical psychologists, who highlight that opportunities to write expressively can reduce stress and improve health. However, it is also essential to recognize that our attempts to support students' healing through writing can easily backfire if we do not inform ourselves about trauma-sensitive approaches to writing instruction. Thus, perhaps Haruki Murakami summed it up best when he said, "In the end, writing is not a full step toward self-healing, just a tiny, very tentative move in that direction" (Smith, 2019).

TEACHING WRITING IN TRAUMA-SENSITIVE WAYS

In what follows, we describe how—and why—three strategies for teaching writing could get implemented in trauma-sensitive ways: studying writers' processes, assigning multigenre and multimodal tasks, and holding writing conferences.

Studying Writers' Processes

A central finding in work on trauma-sensitive literacy instruction and culturally responsive-sustaining pedagogies is that students must build a sense of competence if they are to develop as writers (Alim & Paris, 2017;

Kane & Savitz, 2022; Ladson-Billings, 1995; Lee, 2007; Moll et al., 1992; Moje, 2015). One way to help students to build competence in writing is to support students to understand that writing is a process, and that they can find processes that work for them.

The idea that writing is a process became a focus of cognitive science research in the late 1970s and early 1980s (Flower and Hayes, 1980). The major insight of this research was that writing is an iterative and recursive process in which writers constantly make decisions according to the expectations of the task and their knowledge of the audience. Since then, process writing instruction has become the "primary paradigm" for teaching writing in U.S. schools (Pritchard & Honeycutt, 2006, p. 277). More recent research underpins the importance of writing for authentic purposes and audiences and ensuring that students spend extended time composing about a coherent topic (Graham & Harris, 2019).

Sometimes, teachers interpret process writing instruction to mean that teachers should devote an instructional day to prewriting on Monday, drafting on Tuesday, revising on Wednesday, editing on Thursday, and publishing on Friday (Whitney et al., 2008). However, this depicts writing as an orderly, lockstep procedure through which writers travel, a misrepresentation of writing. Instead, writing is iterative and recursive, meaning that writers might prewrite for years before putting pen to paper (Mattison, 2017), or they might share their work multiple times, deciding later to return to the drafting stage based on feedback. To support students in better understanding writing as a process, students should study the actual writing processes of others—famous and not so famous (Ray, 2007).

For example, I (Britnie) worked for several years with the Lowcountry Writing Project, and we began our time together by researching our favorite authors' writing processes. We learned that Mo Willems's knuffle bunny was not originally a bunny. We found a copy of J. K. Rowling's crimped handwriting in tiny squares, outlining the whole of the *Harry Potter* series. We learned that Ray Bradbury typed *Fahrenheit 451* on a rented typewriter in UCLA's library, where it cost 10 cents to rent the machine for 30 minutes. C. S. Lewis is said never to have used a typewriter, as the clacking of the keys affected his ability to hear the rhythm of the words. Lewis read every sentence aloud. Maya Angelou rented a hotel room by the month, took all the pictures off the walls, and refused to allow the staff to change the sheets—the room was for writing and feeling only, she said. No distractions. Fortunately, since writers love to write, the internet is replete with articles and interviews in which authors describe their processes. By researching a favorite author's writing processes, students will find their nuggets and curiosities and generate ideas on how to get started or what to do when they get stuck.

From the perspective of trauma-sensitive writing instruction, studying writers' processes is important because—through this practice—we can support students to build a sense of competence as writers. As mentioned in

Chapter 1, research highlights that historically marginalized students need opportunities to understand themselves and their experiences as academically valued and valuable—that is, to build a sense of academic competence (Alim & Paris, 2017; Kane & Savitz, 2022; Ladson-Billings, 1995; Lee, 2007; Moll et al., 1992; Moje, 2015). Building students' academic competence is essential for all students, but especially for those who have experienced or are experiencing trauma, because trauma can undermine students' self-efficacy (SAMSHA, 2014), and writing is frequently an area in which students lack a sense of agency or self-efficacy (Boscolo & Gelati, 2019). As we know, writing can be intensely complex and vulnerable work (Dutro, 2019), yet students often spend little time writing extended texts in schools (Applebee & Langer, 2011; Graham & Harris, 2019).

Let's step into Dr. Stacey Reece's high school English classroom to see how she expertly builds academic competence in a writing classroom:

> When students get to me for their sophomore year, one thing I always introduce at the beginning of the year is that we are a community of writers. After I introduce our writing units, I usually hear the same refrain. It goes something like, "[moan] I hate writing," or "I'm a terrible writer." Even after all my assurances that they are writers and they can write, I'm still met with skepticism. Why should they believe me? They don't even know me yet. Actions speak louder than words, so it's time for me to act when I see them in the next class.
>
> The first thing we do as a group is brainstorm what "good" writing looks like; I ask them what they think, and then I record their answers on the whiteboard. Throughout my 30 years as an educator, I've found that students have specific, concrete ideas about this. Most of their answers are based on academic writing. By the time our brainstorming session is over, written on the board are things like "engages the reader," "uses correct punctuation," and "indents paragraphs." After this discussion of "good" writing, I show them a Tweet and ask if it's "good" writing. They almost always say no. Then I show them a paragraph. They almost always say yes. Then I show them a list of items I want to pick up at Target. It's written on the back of an envelope. I ask if that is "good" writing. Now they don't know what to think. Silence fills the air until one student, in a faint, questioning voice, says, "Yes?" When I ask the student to explain, they say, "Because it's things you want to get?" This comment really makes me smile because the student is right—good writing does what you want it to do.
>
> I always begin a new year with personal narratives. These allow students to write about a topic they're familiar with (a person or event that has impacted them in some way) in a format of their choice. They have complete control over this; they can choose a traditional paragraph

form, a poem, or a multimodal format. Most of our mini-lessons cover how to show rather than tell. We use web maps with the event/person in the center and sensory details and emotions around it. We read and annotate various memoirs and narratives from others, focusing on craft. To reinforce the idea that we are all writers, I always write my narrative and share it with them. They can see how writing is a process, how it's okay not to get it right the first time, and how receiving feedback helps. As a matter of fact, when I tell them to have a rough draft ready to go for workshop, I always ask the question, "Is your rough draft good writing?" It takes a few times, but soon they begin to answer, "YES!"

Workshop day revolves around revision. To begin the class, I project my narrative on the board, identify the parts I'm having trouble with, and solicit feedback from the students. By doing so, I invite them to join me in writing rather than me dictating what they should write. Additionally, it's a model for them of what revision consists of. After we revise mine, students can choose from several "help stations," where they can collaborate with others to discuss and receive help on specific issues related to writing. Help stations usually include word choice, punctuation, organization, wordiness, and flow. I don't put time limits on stations; instead, I want students to stay at a station for as long as they need.

After about 45 minutes, we reconvene to discuss the most helpful feedback. Students are encouraged to recognize others who helped them make their writing more impactful. I've found that this floods the room with positivity, builds community, and increases students' self-esteem regarding writing. Knowing that their feedback was helpful to another goes a long way in showing students that they *are* writers.

Finally, we end with what Penny Kittle calls "beautiful words." I invite students to share, anonymously, on a Google Form their favorite line(s) from what they've written. I then compile them into a document and show them off. Students love to see their words displayed. I go through as many as I can, commenting on the beauty in what they've written. I also ask permission from them to display these wonderful words on our class website. Students often come to me after class and tell me they never knew they could write and are excited to finish the narrative. All in all, it's one of the most positive experiences of the year.

To end, I'd like to share some of the beautiful words my sophomores have written:

- The sun was high, the dirt was flattened, and we discussed the universe.

- Heat. All I could perceive was the blistering heat beating against my temple. Beads of sweat trickled continuously down my face, and my body felt uncomfortably damp. The sun's scorching rays streamed through the squalid windows, heating up the aluminum Floor.
- The rotten wooden walls drowned out the sunlight, and the cobwebs seemed to be dripping out of crevices.
- "Do you have at least a B- average?" the principal asked, already knowing my grades consisted of only vowels.
- In that moment, the little bit of dignity I had left snapped like a rubber band that had been stretched too far.

The sense of community that the personal narrative unit provides sustains us throughout the year. For every other writing unit we do, students know we're in it together. They encourage each other, assist each other, and celebrate each other, and it all starts with something they didn't realize they liked and were really good at—writing. Yes, they build confidence in their abilities, but they also recognize that their stories matter and have something to say that's worth listening to. Instilling this sense of voice is at the heart of everything we do.

As fellow ELA teachers, you may recognize the response from Dr. Reece's students: moaning and groaning. Despite this inauspicious start, Dr. Reece helped students develop an individual and collective sense of their competence as writers by positioning them as knowledgeable and leveraging what they already know. For example, she began the year with personal narratives because the narratives of students' lives are already something they know. She also asked kids to brainstorm what good writing is, based on their world knowledge. Thus, from the moment they arrived in class, students were treated as people with great and valuable knowledge that they could draw upon to succeed academically. Later in the unit, students were again positioned as knowledgeable and academically valued when they anonymously posted their favorite lines to a class website.

We suggest that studying writers' processes can also build academic competence. By studying writers' processes, we can normalize struggle and frustration as integral aspects of the writing process. One of Britnie's favorite ways to do this is to ask students to read Lorrie Moore's widely anthologized—and hilarious—essay, "How to Become a Writer," and Anne Lamott's wonderful chapter on her writing process, called "Shitty First Drafts." Lamott (1994) recounts in granular detail just how shitty her first drafts are: "The whole thing would be so long and incoherent and hideous that for the rest of the day I'd obsess about getting creamed by a car before I could write a decent second draft" (p. 25). However, Lamott (1994) also points out that first drafts are an absolute necessity because you can never get to the great writing, or even the passably mediocre writing, until you have written the "down draft"—that hastily scribbled haze of half-formed madness that must be released before the thoughtful writing can come out. Showing students the misfires and follies of "real" writers can help them see their mistakes and frustrations not as a final commentary on their worth as writers and human beings but simply as part of the process. Even great writers experience these frustrations.

To normalize frustration and missteps, students also need to see more than just the work of famous, successful writers, which is—by definition—presented in its most polished and pristine form (Kane & Savitz, 2022). They also need to see models of work in progress, which means that, as teachers, we must make our unfinished, unpolished, imperfect writing available to students. Showing in-progress work gives students access to the ways of thinking that lead to effective writing, which is essential from the standpoint of intellectual growth. Affectively, students need to see what a writer's resilience looks and sounds like. This is particularly poignant for young writers, as much research has highlighted that students' resistance to writing may be rooted in a history of frustration and/or failure (Gallagher, 2011). Thus, studying writers' processes can give students access to writing as a cognitive and affective process, which students need to build a sense of competence about themselves as writers.

Assign Multimodal and Multigenre Tasks

Another opportunity for us, as trauma-sensitive writing teachers, is to assign writing tasks that are multimodal, multigenre, or multisensory.—Multimodal texts are texts in which more than one sense is activated for engagement and is thus received through multiple avenues or modes. The word multimodal is often associated with digital texts, and multimodal texts are often digital, like a podcast or a TikTok video. Until recently, the printing press had limited English language text to a line of words arranged using visual alphabetic symbols that form words, sentences, and paragraphs, usually black letters on a white medium or page. With improved publishing technology, texts now can easily be arranged in nonlinear ways with pictures, graphics, video, sounds, and in some cases, smells. That said, some pre-digital texts, like political cartoons and picture books, are multimodal, because they convey meaning through color, graphics, and text.

Leading experts on writing instruction have long held that providing students space to imagine the genre(s) and mode(s) through which they might express themselves is essential for students to learn to write well (Gallagher, 2011; Ray, 2007), and studies on trauma-sensitive writing instruction agree (Dutro, 2019; Fisher et al., 2020; Siegel-Acevado, 2021. As Dutro (2019) points out, when students write in multiple genres, their "ideas and connections [can] proliferate. Those proliferations include invitations to draw on life-experiences, including the very hardest stuff of life, as resources for school literacies" (p. 30). Thus, writing in multiple genres and modes can encourage students to draw on multiple sources for inspiration, which may—or may not—include their experiences of trauma.

Another advantage of assigning composition tasks in various genres or modes is that it offers opportunities for students to exercise agency through choice. I (Britnie) often tell my teacher education students that adolescent literacy research is almost boring in its gong-like insistence that choice in reading and writing topics is motivational (Jacobs, 2008). One reason is that making choices allows us to exercise our sense of agency, which is essential for students who have or are experiencing trauma since the trauma is often rooted in a loss of agency. As Siegel-Acevado (2021) puts it, telling a "complete, complex, coherent story":

> . . . transform[s] the writer from a victim into something more powerful: a narrator with the power to observe. In short, when we write to express and make sense, we reclaim some measure of agency. (n.p.)

Also, teaching students to write in multiple genres or modes is increasingly necessary in a rapidly globalizing and digitized world (Moje, 2015). An entire subfield in literacy studies, called disciplinary literacy, continues to highlight that students must be able to read and compose a variety of genres that go far beyond the five-paragraph essay: Students need to compose graphs, charts, infographics, posters, analyses of primary source documents, mathematical argumentation, and letters to the editor that showcase academic thinking (e.g., Moje, 2015; Ortlieb et al., in press; Rainey, 2017; Siebert et al., 2016; Spires et al., 2020). In addition, the digitization of our culture means that composition takes multitudinous, hybrid forms, from Twitter feeds and TikTok videos to letters to the editor, political cartoons, and academic articles.

Finally, allowing students to select the topics they will write on allows them to experience the power of writing beyond its utility for expressiveness. Dutro (2019) gives an example of an elementary school student whose older sister, who was 12 years old at the time, was pregnant. When given a chance to choose a research topic, this student decided to research how she might help her sister to care for a baby in the first year of life. Thus, by broadening what counted as writing in her classroom, students had opportunities to discover information relevant and valuable to their lives. From this perspective, all writing—regardless of genre—ultimately stems from our autobiographies. This is not only acceptable but commendable. Dutro (2019) differentiates this kind of autobiographically informed topic selection from examples of classroom instruction in which teachers offer a constrained set of choices from much safer lists, often because this makes teachers more comfortable. For instance, teachers may ask students to write about a favorite animal because it offers students some choice, ensures that students' work is related to a common theme, and it keeps more visceral, sometimes intimidating, topics out of the classroom (Dutro, 2019; Haberl, 2019).

However, students' multimodal compositions, often created in genres not necessarily associated with academia, can become opportunities for both students and teachers to learn relevant and important information about our lives outside of school. In the vignette below, I (Britnie) share an example from my time as a 9th-grade ELA teacher:

> On a Tuesday afternoon, I sat up straight at my desk, pen and rubric in hand, ready to hear my students' research presentations. All around the room, students unfurled their carefully constructed posters. Some of the posters had eye-catching titles. Some had well-organized headings. Most of them even included reasonably accurate MLA citations. Still, I swallowed, biting my nails. Were the pictures insensitive? I wasn't sure. Students started taping their posters to the walls: Suddenly, we were surrounded by facts about cutting or nicotine, depression, neglect, rape, domestic abuse, depression, drug abuse, sexual harassment, alcohol abuse, and suicide. My eyes darted to the door. I wondered what the principal would say if she walked by and saw so many disturbing headings, decorating the room in the same way my 7th-grade teacher had displayed our reports on golden retrievers, greyhounds, and corgis. I cleared my throat, unsure if this instructional plan had been a good one: I had asked students to create informational texts recognizing the signs of specific types of hardship that often arise during adolescence and how to support those who experience them. Students were allowed to choose any topic they wanted. Their choice could be inspired by the novel we were reading, Laurie Halse Anderson's *Speak*, or not. They just had to choose something that mattered to them and teach us about it. I bit my nails, glancing from my rubric ("Students have evaluated the credibility of sources.") to a particularly gruesome picture of cutting. I read the bullet points nearby: Apparently, in its more extreme forms, burning can be categorized as a form of cutting. I swallowed again.
>
> My students began. I struggled to keep up with their shocking facts and figures—the average age of students' first cigarette, the amount of time it takes brain cells to recover after five drinks, and the percentage of girls and women sexually harassed before the age of 16. Soon enough, my room was awash in percentages, hotline numbers, and information. This particular selection of information seemed hard but also relevant to students' lives and, therefore, important. I leaned back, overwhelmed, squinting into my students' faces: Were my students okay through this? Was anyone crying? Anyone pale or squeamish or struggling? But no—they were alert, interested, leaning forward, asking questions.

I, too, leaned forward, returning my attention to the group currently presenting. They were describing what to do if someone tells you they are suicidal. I cleared my throat, rearranging the rubrics on my lap. Don't try to rationalize with your friend, my students said. Don't try to talk him out of it. Just listen. Just hear him. Don't list all the reasons life is worth living; don't tell him that his life is actually quite good by comparison to others less fortunate. Don't remind him that he has loving parents, an overweight cat, a love of Jimmy Buffett, and a best friend who couldn't hit the broadside of a pool ball no matter how many hours the two of you spent together playing pool in the basement. When I next looked at my rubrics, I noticed that my pen was shaking, like my hands. I couldn't steady them. My God, I thought. Everything I had said to my friend—everything—had been exactly wrong. I squeezed my eyes shut, grateful—so grateful—that, ultimately, my friend had not followed through with this most terrible of plans. Still, I imagined myself pleading with some unseen authority, trying to excuse myself for the ways I had violated every bullet point on my students' poster: "I didn't know," I thought. "I didn't know how to react. I didn't know what to say."

Through tears now, I studied the room once more. I didn't know how to respond, but I decided these kids would. I thought about my middle school foray into researching my favorite dog breed, but my report on American Eskimo Dogs now seemed silly, a little futile. Of course, after this one set of presentations, my students would not memorize statistics on common signs of depression or the phone numbers for domestic abuse hotlines. Instead, they would know how to use the internet to find reliable information about issues that press upon their lives. Perhaps the internet would become, for them, more than just a device for scrolling through Insta. Maybe school would become a place that could be trusted to teach my students things they might need to know. Perhaps this unit would leave my students better prepared for the hardships life has to offer.

In their recent position statement on strong writing instruction, the National Council of Teachers of English (2022) highlights that the role of writing teachers is to "advocate for writing instruction that . . . invites students to become writers who (1) write for authentic purposes and (2) make authentic choices about processes and products" (n.p.). In the example above, students could choose their topics and write for an authentic audience—in this case, their peers. Of course, I could also have provided a choice in the genre, adding perhaps an infographic or podcast to the list of possibilities, but this is one example of how students might use more than one mode to create compositions that communicate information that they—and an audience of their peers—find to be useful and relevant. Students may very well find information about the most complex stuff of life to be useful (Dutro, 2019; Haberl 2019).

But Where's the Trauma in This Example of Trauma-Sensitive Writing Instruction?

As you may have noticed, students wrote about trauma in this example, but they weren't writing about their own trauma and they weren't writing expressively. In Dr. Reece's earlier vignette, in which she built a community of writers by positioning students as knowledgeable, we don't know whether students were writing about trauma. This begs the question: Can trauma-sensitive writing instruction proceed if no one is writing about pain, secrecy, or shame? The answer is yes, yes, one thousand times yes. Research on trauma-sensitive writing instruction is crystal clear on this point (Day, 2019; Dutro, 2019; Fisher et al., 2020). Students should never be required to write about trauma: Part of what makes trauma traumatic is that it leads to a loss of agency. If we pressure students to divulge specific life experiences, we rob them of the agency we are helping them to develop. As Dutro (2019) explains, "Making intentional space for stories of trauma is always posed as invitation, *never* requirement" (p. 30). As teachers, we can support students in building resilience without expecting disclosure. Research on trauma-informed writing instruction (which is closely related to trauma-sensitive writing instruction) has noted that "most trauma-informed principles and practices don't rely on disclosures anyway . . . the foundational trauma-informed principles such as safety, trust, collaboration, and so on are generally healthy and respectful principles appreciated by all individuals, regardless of whether they claim a traumatic past" (Day, 2019, p. 152).

On the other hand, Dutro (2019) points out that students should feel welcome to write about their trauma should they wish to do so. She argues that, in trauma-sensitive literacy instruction, teachers invite children to "draw on the fullness of their lives as a welcome resource for school literacies" (p. 31) and to give children opportunities to "see their life experiences, including trauma, as part and parcel of what matters in school" (p. 31). We see this as another example of how teachers can help students build their academic competence: by showing them that their lives and personhood matter and are vital to their literacy learning. It also, importantly, teaches an essential meta-lesson about writing: that writing, too, can serve purposes outside the narrow ones suggested by the near omnipresence of five-paragraph essays. Thus, our primary directive here is to invite students to write or compose about what matters to them deeply—and we should recognize that there may be some students who want and need to write about their trauma. Because we are working to help students develop agency and resilience in their own lives, we must also make space for students to tell their traumatic stories, should they choose to do so.

In the following vignette, Lindsey Blustein describes how she uses poetry as a means through which students might write about trauma, should they choose to do so. Of course, poetry is common in English classrooms, but the focus is often on helping students replicate particular poetic structures rather than capitalizing on the capacity for self-expression inherent in the genre.

> April celebrates National Poetry Month, and most ELA classrooms are teaching some poetry unit at this time. Each year during this month, I allow my 8th-grade ELA students to engage in a poetry project where students write their poems and perform them to an authentic audience at a school-wide poetry night event. In collaboration with the school literacy interventionist, students begin by receiving the prompt, "Where Am I From and Where Am I Going?" and are asked to write a poem of ten lines or more answering the two questions.
>
> I teach in an urban school system where about half of our students identify as Caucasian, and more than half identify as people of color. This poetry project allows students to discuss their identities and where they are from, literally and metaphorically. They write about the town they live in, places they may have lived before, or even where their ancestors or family may be initially from. The writing aims to be an opportunity for students to examine their identities currently on the surface and deeper ones that expand generationally. For instance, students may be from a city in Connecticut, but metaphorically they discuss ideas around race, ethnicity, and past experiences that have shaped them into who they are today. These open writing parameters support trauma-sensitive literacy practices because it is cathartic for students to share and communicate their experiences, identity, and emotions about who they are. Students choose and control how much they are comfortable sharing with their teacher and peers or even a larger audience if they decide to participate in the poetry night event.
>
> When discussing "where am I going?" students are invited to set goals for their future, discuss their dreams, and where they see themselves as they grow older. Middle schoolers look at models from past students, examples from well-known poets, and song lyrics from famous rap artists.

As this vignette and the one before it point out, in trauma-sensitive writing instruction, students are given opportunities to make choices about what they write about, and they can explore the advantages of many genres and modes of communication.

Use Writing Conferences to Respond to Students' Writing Responsibly

For me (Britnie), inviting students to share their trauma in an academic setting is probably the most terrifying prospect of this book. Once the trauma is there, on paper, screen, or podcast, what do we—as responsible, ethical educators—do with it? Unfortunately, the answers are not always clear-cut. The first thing to remember is that teachers are not counselors. As we will discuss, it is not our role to diagnose trauma, and attempting to do so can even be unnecessary. However, as humans and educators, we owe our students authentic responses to their work. We owe our students feedback.

For many, the term *feedback* conjures an image of multiple cups of coffee as you scratch determinedly away at 150 papers, eyes bleary with blue light until you can no longer see the "awk" that you are scrawling in the margins. In that case, we hereby permit you to save your eyesight. Many excellent books are already available about providing high-quality feedback. One of Britnie's favorites is McGee's (2017) *Feedback That Moves Writers Forward*, as well as Carl Anderson's (2000) book on writing conferences. Both books offer deep insight into important practices for providing feedback in the writing classroom, and we recommend diving into them. Both Anderson (2000) and McGee (2017) highlight a central finding about how feedback—even thoughtful paragraphs of enlightened encouragement and critique—will be far less helpful if it only crops up a month after you've received a giant stack of polished pieces in your inbox. Seriously. We must stop doing this. It makes us crazy, and there are much more efficient and beneficial ways to provide feedback to students.

We know, we know: Grading papers after they are submitted is both commonplace and expected. But, research firmly corroborates that this is one tradition with which we can dispense (McGee, 2017). Instead, feedback should always be ongoing, in dialogue with students throughout the writing process (Anderson, 2000). We must find ways to give students little bits of feedback—little bits of response—along the way; otherwise, we are missing invaluable opportunities to help students authentically engage with their work. This is even more important in trauma-sensitive literacy instruction because students' testimonies deserve thoughtful, critical witnesses (Dutro, 2019).

One way to bear witness to students' stories while addressing their academic need for feedback is to use writing conferences. A writing conference, similar to a reading conference, is a brief interaction with a single student in which teachers (1) ask the student to describe the writing work they are trying to accomplish; (2) decide on a single learning objective that will help the writer write this piece and many pieces beyond; and (3) give students an example of what a new approach might sound like on the page, which Anderson calls "writing in the air" (Anderson, 2000). Ideally, every student can spend 3 to 5 minutes with their teacher, focused on students' individual writing, at least once every other week. Thus, writing conferences fulfill one of the primary requirements of high-quality feedback: They are ongoing and continuous (Ball, 2006). From the perspective of trauma-sensitive writing instruction, writing conferences are especially valuable because they give students a chance to describe what they want to accomplish with a piece, thereby highlighting students' agency in authorship (Siegel-Acevado, 2021).

Writing conferences also give teachers a chance to talk with students, one on one, about their writing. Research is clear that this is among the greatest benefits of the writing conference (Ball, 2006). Yet, this benefit can occur only if we take special care to learn how to respond when working with students who have written about their own—or others'—experiences of trauma. Trauma experts first recommend that students' experiences must always be validated, and we must take an asset-based perspective when working with students themselves (Day, 2019; SAMSHA, 2014). Such responses might include normalizing students' responses to experiences of trauma so they feel neither blamed nor shamed. As Day (2019) points out:

> In part, that means avoiding the tendency to pathologize survivors' responses to trauma as "symptoms," implying that something is wrong with the individual; instead, clinicians insist on asking not "what is wrong with you" but "what happened to you" and viewing any "symptoms" as logical adaptations that help the individual cope with adverse, stressful circumstances . . . (p. 151)

To normalize students' responses to trauma, teachers must know common coping mechanisms for trauma, as discussed in Chapter 1. Teachers also must know when to seek additional help from mental health professionals, which will be discussed in Chapter 7.

Elizabeth Dutro (2014, 2019), a leading scholar on trauma-sensitive literacy instruction, also emphasizes that our responses to students' stories of trauma must always be reciprocal: writing can be a powerful form of testimony, and testimony deserves critical witness, as discussed in Chapter 4. Teachers, too, must share difficult experiences, and these responses must include "compassion, connection, and the sense of being entwined with others" (Dutro, 2019, p. 30). We must never act like students are broken and traumatized while we, as teachers, are the healers. We cannot heal others. We are not saviors. We just aren't. We too are hurt and incomplete.

Thus, when students share deeply cut facets of their pain, empathy is the primary tool at our disposal. However, here too we must be thoughtful: In trying to be empathetic, the temptation may be to identify with students' stories of trauma and pain. However, we must not over-identify with students' experiences or assume that our experiences, which may seem similar from an outside perspective, are "the same." For example, Dutro (2019, 2014) recalls speaking to a young student about his sadness—his brother had recently been incarcerated. Dr. Dutro, too, has an imprisoned brother, and she describes the temptation to define her own experience and her student's as the "same." She recalls thinking that she could alleviate some of his burdens by sharing the load of her student's pain.

However—and this is one of the wisest and most important parts of her work—Dutro realizes that for her, a white woman and tenured professor at a flagship university, divulging that her brother had been incarcerated has a very different social impact than it does for her students, who were, at the time, primarily children of color growing up in impoverished urban and suburban areas. For her students, a brother in jail meant they and their families had become yet another instantiation of long-held, negative, and impactful stereotypes that could influence society's view of them and people who look like them. When Dutro tells acquaintances about her brother, she notes that the reaction is typically one of surprise—even shock; it's a curious detail that has no bearing on her current life or future life chances. Not so for students of color living in poverty. Thus, Dutro insists, we are not just witnesses to children's trauma. We must be critical witnesses, aware of how society interprets trauma along very different trajectories, depending on our race, culture, ethnicity, gender, religion, financial status, and other characteristics. We must listen to students and normalize their experiences and coping mechanisms, but we do not define those experiences as "the same" as ours.

Dutro's (2019) findings about the importance of compassionate, humane responses to students' work dovetail with research Britnie has done on how English teachers learn to provide feedback to writers (Kane, 2016, 2020,. To study this, I once hired and trained actors to play students who, in writing conferences, were resistant to revision. (Yes, this was delightful and fun!) Writing conferences are interactive; you can't plan a script for them—each English teacher said something slightly different in response to the actor-student. However, regardless of what the teacher said, the actor's job was to hit on four main ideas: "I'm not a writer"; "I'm done"; "I did revise—I added commas and stuff"; and "I hate writing." The actors were instructed to make only surface-level edits in response to teachers' promptings. The actors followed through, and teachers left these simulated writing conferences exhausted and frustrated.

I'm sure you can empathize. No amount of explaining, modeling, rationalizing, begging, or cajoling led "students" to change anything beyond a comma. Except for one thing: responding to students' writing as human readers. "Wow," one teacher said, "when you wrote about the *click-click* of the roller coaster rising higher, I felt like I was there with you. I was nervous, too. I loved the *click-click* part. And over here, too, this made me feel. . . ." This was the only time an actor sat up, the only time he was interested in what the teacher was saying. Even though our actor was trained not to do anything beyond adding commas and had not written the essay under discussion, he was suddenly listening. "But over here," the teacher said, "at the beginning, where you say, "On my summer vacation, there were four people in my family," I don't get that same sense of nervousness. Can you make the beginning build to that same sense of nervousness of the *click-click* so I can experience the Top Thrill Dragster roller coaster with you? Maybe you could . . ." and the teacher gave just one or two quick ideas. And do you know what our actor said, the same actor who had repelled and rebuffed, refused and recoiled from a constant barrage of feedback from nearly 30 teachers? He said, "Yeah. I could do that. That would be cool." He said that because even this kid, hired to say he would not do it, could not say anything different: Real responses to our thinking, to our lives, are invaluable, and that is the first thing that writers need from us as teachers—regardless of the topic.

Day (2019), who has studied feedback for writers writing about trauma, notes that the best approach is "active, empathetic listening" (p. 221) and responses that include

- Open-ended questions that avoid guiding students to particular answers
- Invitations to elaborate on details regarding their perspective
- Reflective statements to check that the listener has understood correctly
- "I" statements, especially when there is conflict
- Affirmation, expressions of empathy, and avoiding shaming/blaming language
- Humility, especially a willingness to hear out another's perspective and question personal biases
- Respect, especially for cultural and linguistic differences
- Privileging nondirective problem-solving approaches (Day, 2019, p. 165)

Overall, we need to think about the following when we give feedback to students. We should

1. Know common coping mechanisms for trauma so we can better understand students' responses, as discussed in Chapter 1.
2. Invite, but do not expect, disclosure—this is the student's choice.
3. Be mindful that every person in the classroom—including you—needs to be positioned as both the listener and the one in need of listening.
4. Approach students and their writing from an asset-based perspective: What do students already know from their lives and culture(s) that they are leveraging?
5. Respond as a human reader who came to the piece with a specific purpose: What piques your interest? What makes you want to

know more? Where is your purpose for reading fulfilled by the writing, and where could it be better addressed?

6. Understand that students' experiences of trauma are idiosyncratic but that traumatic events may carry with them a sense of social risk for students, especially when those experiences align with negative stereotypes or deficit thinking about students from particular racial, gendered, socioeconomic, or other historically marginalized demographic groups.

CONCLUSION

Our discussion of trauma-sensitive writing instruction highlights that the assumption that writing can be cathartic is borne out—at least in lab settings. However, classrooms are not labs, so we must interpret these results with hopeful caution. We should invite students to write about their experiences of trauma, should they choose to do so, but we cannot require it, as this would rob students of their agency as literal authors of their own lives. Instead, students experiencing trauma, in particular, need opportunities to exercise their authorial agency, so we should give students choices in writing. Fortunately, even if students choose not to write about trauma per se, instruction can still be trauma sensitive. We suggest three potential strategies for trauma-sensitive writing instruction: studying writers' processes, assigning multimodal and multigenre tasks, and using writing conferences.

Students should study writers' processes because it underpins writing as a process, of course, but also because it can help students to build academic competence by showing students that writers struggle, lose their way, and write terrible first drafts (Lamott, 1994). Students should have opportunities to write in multiple modes and genres because it supports them in making authorial choices and because it can show students authentic writing for real purposes in their lives. Finally, we suggest writing conferences because they allow teachers to have human, one-on-one interactions about the topics of students' writing, which are—hopefully—important to them. In the next chapter, we discuss critical inquiry as an important aspect of trauma-sensitive literacy instruction in English Language Arts.

CHAPTER 6

Critical Inquiry in TSLI

"I hate watching the news right now."

"Why do they keep killing us?"

"I'm scared to leave my house."

"Why do white people hate us so much?

These were just some of the frustrated, confused, angry, and, at times, terrified feelings Mrs. McGee heard while working with students and teachers across her district. That semester, news had already covered three highly publicized killings of Black men by law enforcement with little to no consequences, leaving classrooms of Black and Brown students and educators running on empty. Class discussions about the justice system's inequitable treatment of people of color fluctuated between venting sessions and what seemed like therapy sessions, often ending in hopeless shrugs and heart-wrenching testimonies.

In the wake of these anxieties, Mrs. McGee and the 8th-grade teachers she coached had to address the reality that their next unit was anchored by a text many consider inadequate at addressing issues of systemic racism and the justice system, *To Kill a Mockingbird.* As described in Chapter 3, Mrs. McGee and the team of teachers decided to supplement the district-required text with essential questions and a text set that allowed students to explore diverse points of view related to the topics.

When it was time for her to update the rest of the unit, she wanted it to address the essential questions shared below and provide avenues for students to express what they had learned and how systemic racism and the justice system affected their lives and many others in traumatic ways. The more she sat and looked through the previous year's lesson plans and a two-week culminating project that led students through writing a literature analysis essay about *To Kill a Mockingbird,* the more uneasy she felt. The spirit of the text set and essential questions the team had put together left her concerned that students would get to the end of the unit and think, "Now what do I do?" or even worse, "Well, now I feel even more terrible." She didn't want to compound any trauma by leaving students to feel hopeless, or like there was nothing they could do to create a more just world. Even more, she wanted students to be able to process on their own terms their feelings about what was happening in their world.

Fortunately, Mrs. McGee was familiar with many trauma-sensitive teaching principles and the precepts of critical inquiry. She knew she could create lesson plans and an inquiry project to validate students' emotional experiences of the world while also supporting them in meeting the academic expectations of the English Language Arts, such as reading literary and nonfictional texts for themes and bias, communicating complex ideas, and making well-reasoned arguments. Mrs. McGee decided to expand students' understanding of systemic racism and justice by designing a critical inquiry project and lessons that allowed them to process their feelings about the topics in ways that could lead to action and hope. After all, everyone, including herself, felt defeated and helpless about the seemingly endless stream of racially motivated murders and the justice system's inequitable treatment based on race.

Mrs. McGee realized that what students needed was committed teachers as both a comfort and support. And they needed teachers who could incorporate their students' genuine interests and concerns into their work so they would have opportunities to build resilience, develop literacy skills, and become capable of critical thinking and argumentation, as the English Language Arts require, so they could become advocates for change in their own lives.

In this chapter, we explore how critical inquiry can support students' conceptually rich learning, literacy development, and ability to become more resilient participants in the political and social worlds in which they live (Spires et al., 2020). While previous chapters provided multiple strategies, this chapter views the creation of a critical inquiry unit as a set of related steps necessary for creating the unit. Therefore, we go into detail for each part and use one teacher vignette throughout this chapter.

CRITICAL INQUIRY AS A TRAUMA-SENSITIVE LITERACY PRACTICE

Teaching and knowledge are not viewed as a set of inert properties to be acquired but instead as a "transaction" between students and texts, personal experiences, and environmental factors (Smagorinsky, 2019). Knowledge is alive with inquiry, interpretation, and argumentation, and students' funds of knowledge and experience play a significant role in the construction of knowledge (Cohen, 2011; Lampert & Graziani, 2009). There is a partnership in a "risky quest for knowledge" that teachers, students, and texts undertake in the classroom (Darling-Hammond, 2016, p. 86), and teachers know that students' thinking must form the backbone and substance of that partnership. Thus, teachers consistently make students' thinking visible by eliciting their affective and academic thinking (Kane, 2020; Windschitl, 2002), teaching students productive ways to dialogue about academic tasks so that collaboration and discussion surface in their thinking. This type of teaching requires students to participate in authentic opportunities to inquire into, evaluate, and analyze the text and the world in which they live.

Critical inquiry provides many benefits and connections to TSLI. Like critical literacy, critical inquiry is considered "problem-posing education, an education rooted in the existential experiences of the people, in which they explore their own immediate surroundings . . . in an attempt to become more present in understanding and reshaping their own reality" (Freire, 1970, p. 11). Thus, in critical inquiry, students work together to pose questions that are relevant to them, that build on their experiences of the world, and that helps them to "understand and reshape reality" (Morrell, 2008).

In answering their genuine questions, students take a critical stance toward a multitude of canonical and current texts to identify and evaluate problems and issues in the text and in their worlds. They formulate reasons for these problems, and—importantly—they consider all of this from diverse perspectives. They must think from the perspective of literary criticism and the standpoint of their autobiographies, using both to bring a critical eye toward powerful institutions, historical events, and cultural belief systems (Beach et al., 2016).

From the standpoint of TSLI, critical inquiry is appealing because it offers students an opportunity for empowerment and resilience. Research has repeatedly noted that one particularly debilitating side effect of trauma is a loss of agency—trauma can bring about the dangerous and encroaching belief that we cannot influence our lives and futures (Fisher et al., 2020). The goal of teaching with critical inquiry is to place agency back in the hands of students, as students are central throughout the process. Ownership of learning and choice is pivotal for strengthening the agency of students experiencing trauma (O' Drobinak & Kelley, 2021; Perry, 2014).

In critical inquiry, students make choices about the questions they want to ask and direct their learning to challenge themselves; they do so because they find the information important and relevant to their lives (Ahmed & Daniels, 2017; Beach et al., 2016; Beers & Probst, 2017; Mirra et al., 2015). Students' empowerment rests in their ability to pose genuine questions that matter deeply to them and in seeing that what they are reading and learning has a use and a purpose in their lives and the lives of others. Students' voices become a significant component of classroom instruction; a student facing a specific hardship or trauma may thus feel more inclined to share their concerns or ask questions, leading them to further discussion and to problem-solve potential next steps. This type of empowerment is especially critical for students who have experienced trauma, as strengthening a sense of agency is vital to developing resilience (Holmes et al., 2018).

Additionally, critical inquiry is characterized by collaboration because students learn by sharing information, perspectives, and experiences (Lave & Wagner, 1991). Thus, students need to interact with one another, and with the teacher, to co-construct knowledge (Vygotsky, 1986). As we have already learned, co-constructing knowledge and learning with peers and teachers requires strong relationships, high self-efficacy, and trust. Students must be comfortable and willing to take the risk of becoming part of the learning process instead of being told what to know, which means they must build trust with their teacher and classmates. Developing and strengthening teacher-to-student and student-to-student relationships are a must, as these relationships impact student learning (Hattie, 2018).

Ensuring a safe, welcoming environment is imperative, given that students experiencing trauma may associate collaborative work with risk. Luckily, with critical inquiry, teachers and students have more opportunities to form relationships based on mutual trust and care, which are central for all teaching but particularly when teachers place students' experiences of trauma at the forefront of their work. With carefully planned and sensitively orchestrated adaptations, teaching for critical inquiry can become a foundation for teaching that supports students—and teachers—who have experienced trauma. In the following sections, we lay the groundwork for this, outlining seven steps for approaching trauma-sensitive critical inquiry in the classroom, giving examples for each step.

GUIDING PRINCIPLES FOR DESIGNING UNITS OF TRAUMA-SENSITIVE CRITICAL INQUIRY

Using Mrs. McGee's classroom as an example, we want to unpack several essential steps for creating a trauma-sensitive critical inquiry unit, offering additional insight, ideas, and strategies.

Choosing a Topic or Theme

Mrs. McGee began planning for her trauma-sensitive critical inquiry unit by analyzing the themes and materials in the mandated upcoming unit for *To Kill a Mockingbird* with the team of teachers she coached. The group reflected on the sentiments their students were sharing during discussions about current news events in class and how students shared their fears, stories of loss and inequities, and the impact of the ways the media represents people of color (whether they were a victim or accused of a crime) compared to whites. After every news update about an ongoing trial, or lack thereof, students asked such questions as: "When will this stop?"; "Why are we treated so differently?"; and "How do I stop being afraid?" The teachers reflected on how their students' comments and the present-day realities of people of color related to the themes of *To Kill a Mockingbird*, the book scheduled to be discussed in their next unit. They decided that students needed a chance to figure out ways to cope and manage their stress and trauma. The group wanted to redesign the upcoming unit based on their students' voices and concerns, extending a way for students to build upon their agency. They thus chose to focus their critical inquiry unit on systemic racism in the American justice system.

Trauma-sensitive literacy instruction includes students' voices as a substantive part of the curriculum (Fisher et al., 2020; O'Drobinak & Kelley, 2021). Plus, students' thinking is central to any ambitious instructional approach (Smagorinsky, 2019; Windschitl, 2002). As the example above shows, the topic or theme of a trauma-sensitive critical inquiry unit can arise organically in response to students' particular experiences and identities and also in response to current events happening within the school, district, community, or globally.

For instance, after a schoolwide trauma, such as a school shooting or student suicide, schools may want and need ongoing discussion with students and school faculty related to their concerns at that moment. Teachers might also choose a topic by looking at particular texts they want to teach through the lens of authenticity, relevance, and adverse childhood experiences. For example, Erika L. Sánchez's novel *I am Not Your Perfect Mexican Daughter* (2017) focuses on Julia's experiences of depression and anxiety after losing her sister in a tragic accident, deciding what she wants in life versus familiar expectations, and learning about her parent's experience crossing into America (and the secondary trauma from the rape of her mom crossing the border). This novel can be a focal point in a unit on immigration, loss, familial and cultural expectations, or related secondary trauma. As we discussed in Chapter 3, literature provides many rich opportunities to explore such topics as grief, abuse, and other trauma and hardship.

Regardless of which avenue teachers take in deciding on a topic, the critical element is the inclusion of student voices and input to understand that they and their experiences are valued. As Dutro (2019) explains, "supporting children in the midst of challenging circumstances also means designing literacy curriculum and instructional practices that invite and value difficult experiences, rather than silencing such experiences as inappropriate for school or rendering them invisible in the texts and talk of classrooms" (p. 5). Students are more likely to be intrinsically motivated to do research and engage in classwork when they are part of the process of designing curricula and lesson plans (Fisher et al., 2020). Thus, as educators, we need to use our "superpower" of listening to our students (Minor, 2018).

Of course, trauma is often a complex topic for students—and, just as frequently, teachers—to discuss, and some students may not be comfortable sharing their fears, let alone experiences of trauma, with the class. As previously mentioned, we may invite students to write down their questions or concerns on a sticky note to allow them to share without speaking out. It is essential not to create an "us" versus "them" mentality, where the teacher appears to look down on students for experiencing trauma or for teachers to justify traumatic experiences based on race or cultural background (Dutro, 2019). It is also critical to remember that chosen topics may be empowering for some and traumatizing for others. Therefore, a potential backup topic is good if the critical inquiry unit centers on a specific theme. It is also beneficial to explicitly address the potential for discomfort so that students understand that feeling uncomfortable with such discussions isn't wrong. It's normal, and—in a trauma-sensitive critical inquiry classroom—it can be productive.

Discussing and Identifying the Conceptual and Procedural Goals

Once the topic is chosen, it's time to consider the learning outcomes or goals of the trauma-sensitive critical inquiry unit. Having clear expectations for each step is vital for all students, but even more so for students experiencing trauma so that all understand expectations related to process, task, time, space, and place (O'Drobinak & Kelley, 2021). Wilhelm and his colleagues (2014), whose work focuses on supporting students in engaging in authentic, meaningful inquiry and learning, note that they begin with identifying both a conceptual and a procedural goal for the unit. A conceptual goal is "what we want students to *know* and be able to explain and justify by the end of the unit" (Wilhelm et al., 2014, p. 24; original emphasis). Its goal is related to the content that students will learn. For example, Mrs. McGee's conceptual goals for her students included helping them to understand what justice means and how systemic racism influences their lives and the lives of their friends, families, and community.

On the other hand, a procedural goal is about "what we want students to be able to *do and* is most often connected to a particular standard" (p. 24). Wilhelm and his colleagues (2014) note that identifying one overarching conceptual goal and one overarching procedural goal helps to focus instruction around a clear and coherent center (p. 24): "[K]nowledge is a network. When educators go after one central goal, all other related goals that are necessary, symbiotic, or in service of that other goal will also be reached, without checking off long lists of standards, which fragments curriculum" (p. 25). Thus, as teachers develop individual lessons, they can choose how specific standards fit under the heading of the two main goals: procedural and conceptual.

As Mrs. McGee and the team of teachers decided to focus on systemic racism and justice, they also reflected on the standards that would be most appropriate for this unit, as well as the conceptual and procedural goals they wanted to focus on as the main work of the unit. Mrs. McGee focused on the following standard: "Delineate and evaluate the argument and specific claims in a text, assessing whether the reasoning is sound and the evidence is relevant and sufficient; recognize when irrelevant evidence is introduced" (CCSS.ELA-LITERACY.RI.8.8; Common Core State Standards, 2010). She selected this standard because argumentation is at the heart of English as a discipline and because making an argument about issues that matter to students is also central to critical inquiry and is based on students coming up with a question that matters to them and using research to take a position on the issue. In critical inquiry, students can offer potential solutions, argue that the issue should be reframed, or share their findings with others who could benefit from learning about systemic racism or the justice system (Beach et al., 2016; Wilhelm et al., 2014). Thus, this standard would be an excellent fit for a critical inquiry unit.

The unit's conceptual goals are to differentiate among definitions of racism, stereotypes, bias, and intolerance, to understand inequities in the justice system, and to have a tool kit for advocating for equitable treatment for all. The procedural goal, as noted above, is related to what students will learn *how* to do. In this case, they will learn *how* to make an argument for at least two specific audiences.

Activating Background Knowledge and Front-Loading

Having selected a topic and conceptual and procedural goals, Mrs. McGee turned her attention to what students needed to know to begin posing a question related to justice that would frame their inquiry projects. She began to consider what information teachers might front-load for the students related to systemic racism and the justice system. Because the team was working with an established unit that they reworked into a critical inquiry unit, it was essential to ensure that the readings and lessons leading up to students posing their questions about the unit topics gave them a foundational understanding of systemic racism and the justice system. After reviewing the lessons for the unit, and the anchor text and text set, it was clear that students would gain knowledge of some BIPOC Americans' experience with the justice system, both as a victim and as the accused, as well as the inner workings of the court system. While the text set and anchor text gave students common background knowledge, they needed to research how the unit topics related to local issues that could affect their personal lives before designing their inquiry questions.

Mrs. McGee located specific websites and organizations to recommend for research. Guided by her conceptual goal for the unit, she delved deeply into the world of local and national legal statistics and websites. She planned for teachers to spend a day supporting students in becoming familiar with these resources and helping them see their relevance. The number of days is not a hard and fast rule; it depends on students' background knowledge, interest level, and the literacy skills and strategies teachers choose to highlight. It is important to note that, although Mrs. McGee curated a list of potential resources by going to well-known organizational websites like the ACLU and the Innocence Project (innocenceproject.org), these often changed as students' curiosity, life experiences, and interests led them to create their inquiry questions.

In addition to sharing content to build students' background knowledge, Mrs. McGee and the team knew they would need to focus on supporting students' development of specific literacy skills. For instance, they wanted to ensure students engaged in closely reading texts as they researched, particularly regarding online research skills. Therefore, they modeled how to determine if an article was credible by doing a quick Google search using the terms "teenagers" and "murder." Opening a couple of the online pieces they found, they walked students through determining the article's author and then assessing the author's background, experience, and research (Leu et al., 2014). They then aided students in checking organizational affiliation to determine potential bias in the research. Teachers also discussed how media outlets might be biased depending on their political leaning. In addition, they taught students to check the dates of the articles to determine if newer information was available. Thus, by using up-to-date, authentic, and digital texts, the team could address several ELA standards related to identifying bias and digital literacy on their way toward achieving the overarching procedural goal of helping students to use research to build an argument.

Once students moved from modeled practice of this skill to independent ability to determine if an article or website may be credible and valid, the team moved on to teaching how they wanted students to annotate the text. Because many of the articles and books that students found to support their research were quite complex with academic vocabulary, the team wanted to ensure that students could document when they had questions as they read. They thus modeled a simple annotation tool for students to use:

? = I need help to understand something shared in this section.
! = This is important information that my group will want to discuss.
+ = I need additional information and will need to research further.
V = The vocabulary term is unknown, or I need support.
* = This information relates to something from another article.

Instruction in many potential skills can be front-loaded at this time, such as teaching text structures or text features so that students understand how to use all information provided in a text. Or you may want to model for students how to use specific graphic organizers to document what they are learning. If there are strategies or skills that only some students need, you could consider pulling small groups aside to support those with specific growth areas. Assessing what students already know or strategies they may need to review is critical, as educators must build a foundational knowledge base to ensure successful inquiry (Fisher et al. 2020). It is also a good time to reach out to experts to gather additional factual information and to consider inviting them to the classroom as guest speakers to share their expertise throughout the unit (Fisher et al., 2020).

Discussing and Creating Inquiry Questions

Creating inquiry questions is vital as the questions guide student investigations. Many ELA teachers organize their unit plans using an overarching essential question that drives the entire unit. However, within a trauma-sensitive critical inquiry unit, teachers choose the overarching topic with student input, as noted in Mrs. McGee's example, so that the locus of control shifts to students, allowing them to articulate their questions to explore and investigate based on their life experiences, questions, and curiosities. Typical requirements for this type of question are that it is open-ended and requires research and exploration of multiple perspectives to inform or solve a problem (Savitz & Wallace, 2016; Spires et al., 2020). The question should be thought provoking and require critical thinking, evidence, and justification to solve (McTighe & Wiggins, 2013). And if the question aligns with traumatic or personal experiences, we want to ensure students' ability to share authentic situations and concerns and collaborate with classmates with similar concerns and curiosities. In other words, the question should require students to develop a deeper understanding of a topic and relate it to issues outside the classroom. The teacher becomes a facilitator of students' learning, where we guide them in asking additional questions and finding answers to those already posed.

At this point in her lesson, Mrs. McGee provided some background information related to systemic racism and justice, some statistics such as the number of people of color incarcerated in their city, and some information on ways to advocate for change; she then asked students to share their questions. She ensured that students could ask questions related to what they were already learning, personal questions, as well as questions related to societal issues. It is important to note that teachers must remind students of the classroom community norms negotiated early in the year and discuss the necessity of being sensitive to each other. Mrs. McGee wanted to set up a healthy conversation around trauma that allowed students to share personal experiences while also being mindful of when the conversation may trigger a student, as discussed in Chapter 4. Because Mrs. McGee and the team of teachers supported conversations related to personal issues and the sharing of self and experiences, and because they had established a robust community classroom environment, she referred to her "out" plan. This plan designated what students should do when they need to step away from the conversation and work if a student appeared to be retraumatized or triggered by the conversation.

Through a brainstorming activity, students determined their lines of inquiry based on the unit, using a modified K-W-L chart, in which students record what they already know, what they want to know, and—after the unit—what they learned. Instead of students starting with what they already knew, however, they filled out a chart with "What I Learned about Justice" and "What I Want to Know about Justice" to brainstorm what they wanted to explore further. They were encouraged to think about local, state, or national issues they wanted to research related to justice. Students came up with inquiry questions about mass incarceration, the war on drugs, and how social media or the news portrays people of color, to name a few. The next step is to look at the 20+ questions asked and determine if multiple students were interested in researching together (Savitz & Wallace, 2016). As inquiry questions were modified and crafted, it was important for all class members to continue asking themselves if the question was directly related to what they wanted to learn and investigate. The group also had to consider whether a given query would have enough depth to require investigation from multiple perspectives and sources. Ultimately, groups were formed in each classroom with inquiry questions such as these to guide their investigations:

- What needs to happen so police don't kill so many people of color compared to white people? What kind of training works?
- How does someone innocent get help when accused of a crime? How can we help people know what to do in these situations?
- Why are prison sentences so different for people of color than for white people convicted of the same crime?
- What can young people do to advocate for changes in the justice system?

Conducting Research/Teacher as Facilitator

In Mrs. McGee's and her team's classrooms, students began researching together once they formed their inquiry groups. Students led their research effort, with the team's help in determining where to find appropriate resources and supplemental information. While researching, the goal was for students to collaborate, talk, share, and start framing answers to their inquiry questions by considering multiple perspectives. They read complex texts, synthesized information, developed academic and specialized vocabulary, and more.

While students' interests and experiences led the way in this process, the teachers had to remember not to leave students alone to flounder and muddle through complicated sheaves of information. Instead, they circulated among each group, using informal—or formative—assessments to note where students needed support and to design mini-lessons around the literacy strategies students needed to develop to succeed (Afflerbach, 2018). Teachers held one-on-one conferences, like those mentioned in Chapter 4, to provide individual student support. For instance, one group struggled to find additional resources, so the teacher brainstormed other search terms. When another group struggled with finding the main details and ideas from their articles, their teacher sat down and retaught them how to identify the who, what, when, why, and how, along with a brief article description. This strategy encouraged students to focus on the article's main points rather than getting bogged down in details.

Other times, when multiple groups needed extra help, the teachers offered whole-class instruction, reteaching a skill or strategy or trying new framing to support their research. For instance, many student groups in one classroom wanted additional support in documenting statistics with their questions, so Mrs. McGee worked with teachers and students using a double-entry journal to document statistics with either questions or findings. Teachers provided whole-class mini-lessons in another classroom when numerous groups required a more robust understanding of identifying and critiquing warrants in a claim. Teachers also understood when someone outside the classroom would best serve as support, leading one teacher to send a student group to discuss their topic with the school principal.

If groups appeared to be doing well on their own, Mrs. McGee and the team of teachers would stop by to ask basic check-in questions to find out where their investigation was going or to help further their thinking. They continued to use the gradual release of responsibility framework (Fisher & Frey, 2014) to ensure that students had proper modeling and practice before moving on to the next group. Ultimately, teachers understood that they must give students enough time to explore, research, and potentially modify their inquiry questions as they learned together and refined an interpretation or solution in response to their question(s).

Additional Resources for Inquiries

A trauma-sensitive literacy classroom provides students with ways to discuss, share, and learn together. Therefore, discussions and research interests may move in unexpected directions. The good thing is that there are many resources and websites that can provide students with valuable and credible information to start their investigations. Of the many useful and trustworthy websites, the nine listed below represent topics related to adversity and resilience for students and teachers.

- RACE: The Power of an Illusion (pbs.org/race/000_General/000_00-Home.htm) is a website that aligns with California Newsreel's three-part documentary on race in society, science, and history. The site provides access to the documentary along with additional resources relating to the developmental history of the social construct of race and makes visible how people experience race and discrimination differently (Demoiny, 2018).

- Learning for Justice (learningforjustice.org), previously known as Teaching Tolerance, seeks to uphold the mission of the Southern Poverty Law Center: to be a catalyst for racial justice in the South and beyond, working in partnership with communities to dismantle white supremacy, strengthen intersectional movements, and advance the human rights of all people. They focus their work in the areas of Culture and Climate, Curriculum and Instruction, Leadership, and Family and Community Engagement. They provide free educational resources (e.g., articles, guides, lessons, films, webinars, frameworks) to help foster shared learning and reflection for educators, young people, caregivers, and all Community members.
- The NY Times Learning Network's Resources for Teaching and Learning (nytimes.com/spotlight/learning-activities-for-students) provides lesson plans, teaching ideas, student opinion questions, picture and film prompts, current events, and much more. Information can sort by discipline or by searching for specific topics. A unique feature is the student opinion section, where students can explore their topic or inquiry and read the questions and responses of other students.
- Facing History and Ourselves (facinghistory.org) is a nonprofit international educational and professional organization that promotes the development of a more humane and knowledgeable society relating to issues of racism, religious intolerance, and hatred. It advocates for students to understand and connect history to their lives to encourage ethical decision-making and understanding of their roles and responsibilities in a democratic society. The website provides teacher resources for implementing discussion and debate in classrooms, fostering empathy and reflection.
- Abolitionist Teaching Network's mission (abolitionistteachingnetwork.org) is to develop and support teachers struggling for educational liberation by utilizing the intellectual work and direct action of Abolitionists in many forms. They provide Resources for Agitators, including podcasts, videos, articles, and research.
- The Gay and Lesbian Alliance Against Defamation (glaad.org) encourages dialogue about the issues LGBTQ people endure in the hope of shaping the narrative and accelerating acceptance. In addition to the stand the organization takes through entertainment, news, and digital media outlets, various briefs and reports are provided ranging in topics from the acceptance of all people to specific instances of LGBTQ people in parts of this country.
- Kids as Self Advocates (fvkasa.org/index.php) is a national, grassroots project created by youth with disabilities for youth. Members provide information and promote discussion based on

their lived experiences, focusing on a Theory of Change. They offer voice and advocacy for youth with and without disabilities by attending public events and hearings. In addition, they provide over 60 tip sheets and guides written by youth for youth.

- Kids' Quest (cdc.gov/ncbddd/kids/index.html), part of the Centers for Disease Control and Prevention, offers interactive and entertaining ways to learn about health issues. First, students take a short quiz to determine prior knowledge and to think about questions they may have. They then receive quick facts and can explore websites and resources, movies, informational video clips, and books to support learning. In addition, the website promotes further inquiry and investigation relating to the topic and the student's school and community. Exposure to this site gives students a resource for exploring issues they may be reluctant to address with teachers or other adults, such as sexual health.
- stopbullying.gov is a federal government website that offers resources on bullying, cyberbullying, and prevention. The organization promotes conversations about bullying, intending to build a safe school environment through a community-wide bullying prevention plan. Resources and information span specific policies and laws, research, and support related to teen dating violence, disabilities and special needs, and prevention. Federal and nonfederal sources are available in research, programs, fact sheets, infographics, and podcasts.

Presenting Information/Action and Advocating

The last step is for students to share their findings with the class or other audiences. One crucial aspect of trauma-sensitive critical inquiry is that units offer opportunities for students to learn how to advocate for and enact change in their worlds (Beach et al., 2016; Wilhelm et al., 2014). The final assessments for a trauma-sensitive critical inquiry unit are thus always authentic and intended to work toward local, community, or world transformation. Because the unit's procedural goal is about learning to make arguments based on multiple perspectives, students end their unit by crafting persuasive arguments based on claims and perspectives found in their research. This type of writing does not mean that students should write five-paragraph essays to share with their class—indeed, many scholars argue that five-paragraph essays can limit students' critical thinking (Hillocks, 2002; Wesley, 2000).

Instead, as was true when students created their questions, it is essential to make space for students' choices on how they show evidence of learning and which audiences they hope to speak to. Providing choice is a pillar of TSLI because it empowers students to make decisions about their learning and leverages the funds of knowledge they bring into the classroom (Moll et al., 1992; Wilhelm et al., 2014). Students become agentic as part of the decision-making process about how *they* want to share their findings and information.

Students in Mrs. McGee's district chose end-of-unit assessments ranging from traditional PowerPoint presentations to more creative approaches such as narrated videos, podcasts, drama re-enactments, or art distributed to others. These teachers ensured that students had authentic audiences, including other students in the school, school personnel, community members, organizations, the local City Council or the State Board of Education, and even global audiences. One way for students to engage with a global audience is by creating TED-Ed clubs where students develop TED Talks, shared on social media platforms (Stedronsky & Hawley Turner, 2020).

The response from students in Mrs. McGee's district was overwhelming. Classrooms suddenly felt like busy newsrooms as students worked furiously to research and create presentations on current topics related to justice and race they felt passionately about. One student made a news broadcast for the younger students at their school about the number of local BIPOC people on trial for crimes with little to no evidence, urging them to write to their local government. Another student wrote a letter to their school administration to persuade them to start an elective or club for political advocacy. Student after student created projects that not only showcased something they were passionate about but which enabled them to demand action.

CONCLUSION

What Mrs. McGee's district experienced should come as no surprise as students learned and demonstrated sophisticated literacy skills and strategies; in asking their questions and finding answers, students were front and center, fully engaged in their learning. Teachers understood that students had questions based on personal and community experiences. They knew students needed a place to raise their questions and to explore their concerns and curiosities (Garcia, 2021).

These teachers understood there was no "right" answer to students' questions and that students wanted—no, *needed*—to understand what was happening, but they needed to figure the answers out in their own ways. In other words, teachers let students guide their learning based on these questions in the hope of understanding the situation and then taking action. Notably, students learned not only to find credible sources but also to analyze biases and missing perspectives. Through this inquiry, students were agentic and empowered—answering questions about social inequities that impact them in the real world (Mirra et al., 2015).

While there isn't a single "how to" for creating these opportunities in our classrooms, as local issues and student interests should guide them, we want to share a few common considerations for this type of teaching. First, as noted throughout this chapter, we must invite students to share their concerns, opinions, and questions about current events at the local, national, and global levels. Then, we must consider texts and themes that overlap with students' inquiries and consider using "the texts that students find and create through their research to teach standards-based reading, writing, speaking, and listening skills" (Mirra et al., 2015, p. 54). Of course, consider who in the community (and beyond, with digital access to potentially anyone in the world) might serve as a resource or guest speaker for students to aid them in exploring their questions (Fisher et al., 2020).

This type of instruction honors long-standing goals of English studies, such as "valuing student perspectives; understanding the experience of others through literature and cultural study; and fostering kindness, thoughtfulness, and justice" (Beach et al., 2016, p. 5). Trauma-sensitive critical inquiry follows theoretical and curricular shifts that change restrictive experiences of students to a focus on student agents who contribute to their own learning process (McLaughlin & DeVoogd, 2004). TSLI can speak directly to students about trauma—their own experiences of it, as well as the experiences of others. Thus, through critical inquiry, students can become more resilient in the political and social worlds in which they live—learning how to advocate for themselves and others (Spires et al., 2020).

CHAPTER 7

Hot Moments—Teacher Self-Care

My philosophy as a teacher is that we must create safe spaces to hear all students' voices, even if some of those voices do not say popular things in society. As a high school ELA teacher, I have been more intentional about addressing uncomfortable societal issues in recent years. These conversations are often about social justice themes or historical contexts that may be troubling for some students. While the topics are not always easy to talk about, they are necessary and relevant in today's social climate. Therefore, I choose to address the challenging topics students have to deal with daily.

To avoid full-blown polarizing arguments among my students, one of my rules before any discussion is that we must listen first. I model this by showing students how to let someone else finish what they are saying, even if I disagree with their ideas or thoughts. Students also know they must support their claims and beliefs with evidence or provide reasoning grounded on facts. Sometimes students can do that, and other times they start to see the weakness in their own argument.

For instance, after the Marjory Stoneman Douglas shooting on February 14, 2018, not far from our school, students needed a space to talk and to feel safe and valued. My classroom became that space for many of them. The day after the shooting, I opened our classroom discussion about the events. I wanted students to have a time and place to speak about their feelings. One student raised her hand and said that the problem was that guns like semiautomatic weapons should be banned because they serve no purpose in our society. I followed it up and asked for her reasoning and evidence. While she discussed and blamed a certain political party, her statements created a significant response from other students—some were very upset, and others agreed. Before this blew into a storm, I reminded students first to listen, before opening up space for students to respond. This prompted a quick discussion on the initial reasoning, with another student stating that the initial claim was not strong, followed by his argument and reasoning. This moved the conversation into consideration of guns being the problem, politicians being the problem, or people being the problem. These differing viewpoints represented the students in my classroom, which means there were also physical and emotional reactions.

At this time, our typically civilized conversations started to unravel because students started to talk over each other. I counted down from five to get their attention, and I addressed that neither side had provided facts to support their claims. They quieted down and searched for at least one piece of evidence to support their stance and to come up with a rebuttal to a point the other side would give.

While students' emotions were high, I wanted them to listen and to focus their emotions on a real-world community collective trauma in a way that also supported their learning and becoming citizens in their world. I wanted my students to practice what they had previously learned about finding reliable sources while they processed this local tragedy. And after about 30 minutes, I invited students to share their findings, articulating their thoughts with reasoned arguments. Some held firm in their beliefs, while others began considering other perspectives. And while my lesson for this day was to engage students in reading *Romeo and Juliet*, this day instead became an opportunity for students to learn how to have difficult conversations and the importance of supporting claims with facts.

—Dr. Carmen Marroquin, High School English Language Arts

Dr. Marroquin's example is one of many we have witnessed in our teaching and working with others, regardless of the age of our students. Students speaking up is part of us valuing their identities, experiences, and traumas in our curricula and relationships with one another, promoting each person to share their vulnerabilities, questions, and differing perspectives with all. TSLI classrooms encourage students to ask questions and gently push back on people's beliefs, which means we must also understand that these moments may be uncomfortable in their complexity. Students may speak out of turn and become confrontational based on their beliefs, compassion for others and events, and personal experiences. Dr. Marroquin prioritized creating safe spaces at the start of the year and students' ability to listen first, evaluate evidence, and finally consider their perspective, even being open to changing their beliefs. While this chapter cannot provide a simple solution for dealing with what we call "hot moments," we offer some places to turn, ideas to consider, and examples of how educators have dealt with hot moments in their classrooms.

HANDLING HOT MOMENTS

Hot moments often occur during classroom activities such as discussion and writing when students share vulnerability, listen and learn from one another, and question personal and others' perspectives. These moments are often tense as students explore their beliefs and assumptions. These can occur "when a student makes a controversial statement, discloses something troubling, or raises a question that requires a sensitive response" (Fisher et al., 2020, p. 67). However, as noted with Dr. Marroquin, how we handle the hot moment matters most for our students and our sanity. Instead of silencing our students, which can lead students to feel shamed or voiceless, we can acknowledge the situation and support and protect all students. In other words, we can take these opportunities to support learning others' perspectives and make these teachable moments. But to do so, we must first have strong, positive relationships with our students in TSLI classrooms.

Building Trust and Relationships

As previously shared, we must consider how we as teachers value diversity and engage students in sharing and learning diverse perspectives to create welcoming spaces where students feel connected to their classroom community, identify as learners, feel valued, and have a sense of belonging (Comber, 2015; Nieto & Bode, 2018). Students knowing they are respected and appreciated no matter who they are tells them it is okay to be worried and that it is also okay to bring their concerns into the classroom. They understand that while a teacher may not experience what they are experiencing, they will be heard and supported to the best of the teacher's ability and that we want to learn who they are and what they are thinking. The classroom community becomes a two-way street of sharing and learning, connecting with others from differing experiences and backgrounds, and respecting others' opinions (Kinloch et al., 2021; Parker, 2022; Ticknor et al., 2021).

In these classrooms, students have a strong connection with an adult and their peers, building resilience for students who have experienced, or are experiencing, a traumatic situation. These relationships are crucial because we know how students experiencing trauma often struggle to develop healthy relationships (Fisher et al., 2020), toggling between their past experiences and emotions and predictions about what will occur next (Cozolino, 2014). When they attempt to decide on whether to trust or not, they may not appropriately deal with the stress or reactions of others because they may have a lower capacity to consider and choose the emotional and cognitive resources necessary to learn and engage with others in healthy ways (Holmes et al., 2018). Therefore, it is easier to diffuse a hot moment when students feel safe and trust one another, because as they experience additional stress dealing with conflicting beliefs, they do not feel threatened by disagreeing with others (O'Drobinak & Kelley, 2021).

Dr. Brené Brown, a research professor at the University of Houston and Endowed Chair at the Graduate College of Social Work, highlights ways that educators can build trust with students in "Braving: The Seven Elements of Trust" (2018). Brown highlights the ways that teachers should treat students and vice versa:

- **Boundaries:** You respect my boundaries, and when you're unclear about what's okay and not okay, you ask. You're willing to say no.
- **Reliability:** You do what you say you'll do. At work, this means staying aware of your competencies and limitations, so you don't overpromise and can deliver on commitments and balance competing priorities.
- **Accountability:** You own your mistakes, apologize, and make amends.
- **Vault:** You don't share information or experiences that are not yours to share. I need to know that my confidences are kept and that you're not sharing with me any information about other people that should be confidential.
- **Integrity:** You choose courage over comfort. You choose what is right over what is fun, fast, or easy. And you choose to practice your values rather than simply professing them.
- **Nonjudgment:** I can ask for what I need, and you can ask for what you need. We can talk about how we feel without judgment.
- **Generosity:** You extend the most generous interpretation possible to the intentions, words, and actions of others. (Brown, 2018, n.p.)

Additionally, teachers can directly ask students how they feel in their classroom and ways to support their learning and resilience. The Abolitionist Teaching Network (2020) recommends asking students these six questions to gather student input in building a trusting relationship with them:

- What can you tell me that helps me better understand you as a person?
- How can I be the best teacher for you?
- How can your school be a place where you feel seen, valued, and excited to learn?
- What matters most to you (e.g., life at school, in your community)?
- How can I support you mentally, emotionally, and in your community?
- What is your love language?

While these are two ways to build trust with students, we recommend reflecting critically on how you build relationships and trust with all your students.

Creating "Rules" for Engagement

One aspect you want to consider is how students should engage with others when they agree, and when they disagree with their classmates or you. These rules or norms for engagement can differ based on how you and your students communicate. For instance, for me (Rachelle), I tend to start the year by negotiating with students our rules and classroom norms. This entails sharing my expectations and how I communicate, and students sharing their thoughts and needs. We then work together to determine our classroom and discussion norms, revisiting them throughout the year to update them as needed, especially as our relationships strengthen.

However, we know that without being in our classroom to witness these conversations with our students, it can be confusing without guidance. And while we cannot provide a specific template or go-to way to create guidelines in your classroom because we believe in negotiating this with your students, you may engage students in similar discussions about expectations, norms, and needs. We recommend starting this conversation early in the school year and to adjust as needed throughout the year and to talk with students about ways for them to let you know if something offensive was said and then how the class can learn and grow together, moving forward in respectful and trusting ways.

Importantly, when inviting students to share and engage in TSLI work, we want to reiterate the importance of a few considerations. First, it is important to have a plan negotiated with students *and* school administrators for what students will do if they feel uncomfortable or upset. Students' safety is a priority that we must ensure, and students must know that this is of utmost importance to us. We also recommend monitoring for any sense of unease noted by students and to have a plan for students to share their concerns privately. Another consideration is incorporating daily or regular check-ins to invite students to share any life updates or how they feel (Homrich-Knieling, 2019). As will be discussed below (see Mandated Reporting), we highly recommend never making a promise not to tell anyone something if students want to share about abuse or neglect.

For those of you who want more concrete ideas on establishing specific guidelines, we direct you to the University of Michigan Inclusive Teaching Hot Moments website (sites.lsa.umich.edu/inclusive-teaching/hot-moments), which provides resources for establishing discussion guidelines, responding to common dialogue blockers, applying dialogic techniques, and handling conflicts in the classroom. While this information is meant for university instructors, it is also applicable and appropriate for middle and high school educators. Their concrete recommendations include the following:

- Take a moment.
- Save it for later.
- Refer to class discussion guidelines.
- Write down thoughts.
- Clarify student comments.
- Depersonalize.
- Provide a basic common understanding.

- Validate student contributions.
- Connect comments to course material and learning goals.
- Share anonymously.
- Facilitate a dialogue.
- Reflect individually or collectively.
- Talk outside of class.
- Connect with your support network.

While we hope that all our students will respectfully and consistently reflect on how others perceive their words and actions, we know this is not always the case. Therefore, the first "hot moment" we want to explore is how Rachel Bolte sets up her classroom and teaches her 9th-grade students the importance of thinking through what they say and not causing harm to others. Importantly, Rachel understands that her 9th-grade students are still learning, as are all of us, which means there will be times when a comment is hurtful without intent. Let's read how she sets students up for healthy dialogue and what she does when something goes awry.

> From the beginning of the year, we practice various academic habits—one of which is academic discourse. First, this looks like me, the teacher, modeling, asking questions, and listening and responding to others. When students ask questions in class, I make space either to answer them now or to ask them if it's ok if we follow up after class. I ask follow-up clarifying questions to ensure I understand precisely what they are asking. This allows learners to know I've heard their question, and it has merit even if we don't have space to go in depth. They then can use this as a model for listening to others and asking clarifying questions throughout the year.
>
> I use seminar-style discussions in my classrooms around topics such as love. We all sit in a circle, and I start with a question to ensure that all voices are heard, at least at the beginning of the discussion. Additional questions follow, some from previous analyses or questions posed during instruction. From there, students respond to their peers using each other's names and building on each other's words rather than just agreeing or disagreeing. When the conversation ends naturally, a new question is posed; however, the discussion is often fruitful, so we seldom make it through all the prepared questions.
>
> For example, we explore healthy and unhealthy relationship characteristics when they read *Romeo and Juliet* as an anchor text in their Literature class. Students reflect and converse with each other to determine whether the characters in the play were in healthy relationships and then reflect on relationships in their own lives. There

> are plenty of awkward silences as students figure out how best to make their point, but I find those silences essential to provide room for all students to engage in the discussion.
>
> Being able to consider how we communicate and what we say is crucial. I try to cultivate a space where all questions are valued by encouraging questions and unstructured talk among students (and the teachers in the space). Inevitably, when questions or comments are insensitive or offensive (these students are 14 or 15 years old, after all), I pause instruction or activity and address it immediately, individually, and as a whole class.
>
> If it is a comment that is hurtful to others or causes harm, I will address it with the whole class to remind all my students of the classroom expectations of respect that we set at the beginning of the year. Then, once all the students start their work again, I will have an individual conversation in the hallway with the student who commented. I explain why the comment was hurtful to others and seek to understand why they said it in the first place. I like to remind my kids that we all make mistakes and can be kinder and more aware of our words in the future. Then, if a particular student was harmed with a comment, I will check in with them individually to see how best to repair the harm. My intent is to make it clear that offensive language is unacceptable and that I have the backs of students whom the offensive comments affect. It takes time, but by the end of the year, our 9th-graders, for the most part, self-correct and make a point to be kind and inclusive (at least in a whole-group setting).

We commend Rachel for considering, planning, and teaching students the protocol and expectations for sharing thoughts—but more importantly, what is needed when we say something that causes harm.

Similarly, when I (Rachelle), recently taught a cultural diversity course for teachers seeking a master's degree in literacy, a discussion ensued about the swastika and the origination of this symbol. As part of the course, during each synchronous online class session, we read realistic hypothetical classroom scenarios from Gorski and Pothini's (2018) book *Case Studies on Diversity and Social Justice Education*. In this book, scenarios can be chosen by social construct (e.g., religion, race, language) or by structural theme (e.g., curriculum and pedagogy, school culture, bias, and bullying) to investigate traditional school policies and practices.

One scenario discussed a child wearing a swastika to school. The students in the scenario were upset with their classmate and shared that it was offensive to them. However, the student wearing the swastika pointed out that the symbol did not represent hatred but was an ancient Hindu symbol and was given to him by his late grandmother. Ultimately, the teacher asked the student to take off his necklace, and they negotiated, agreeing he could wear the necklace underneath his shirt. This scenario provided questions for those reading it to consider the teacher's and students' actions and if they would have taken time in their classroom to discuss the situation more with the class.

My mother was born in a deportation camp after WWII, and I lost family members during the Holocaust, so I was unsettled as I read this scenario. My gut reaction was to side with the teacher, but I was torn because the student wearing the swastika was honoring his culture. As a teacher educator who believes in valuing individual differences and identities and teaching about culturally responsive and sustaining pedagogy, I was unsure how to proceed. While I could have shut the conversation down based on my personal feelings or religious beliefs, I owed it to my students to let them explore, question why, and think through each other's thoughts and reasoning. This hot moment could have prompted a room full of adults to get enraged or even do something drastic. However, as the teacher, it was up to me to step up to the proverbial plate and listen to students' thoughts on all sides of the hexagon.

Thus, for the next 20 minutes, we explored the swastika symbol and others, researching the history and how others define and place value on various symbols. We talked through differing perspectives. While the conversation could have gotten heated and even defensive from me or others, we taught ourselves to listen and to learn from others' cultures and values. We walked away with our own beliefs about symbols such as the swastika but were more prepared for how to handle this type of conversation next time. And while I first regretted using this scenario in class, it taught me a valuable lesson: that language and dialogue hold great power, allowing us to talk through our beliefs, learn from others, and explore complex topics together.

Correcting Our Mistakes Matters

Similarly, as educators, we must also consider what happens when we, as teachers, are well intentioned in planning our lessons but make mistakes. We may not realize that our assumptions are problematic or that our materials or lessons need tweaking to best support our students' lived experiences and expectations of what they want, *need,* to learn in our classroom. Let's then take a moment to reflect on Dr. Brooke Bianchi-Pennington's bravery as she shares vulnerability with us regarding a moment in her English II classroom teaching when she had to stop and question her plan and make immediate changes when her lesson triggered her students.

> Creating space in my sophomore English classroom for students to explore and discuss critical social issues relevant to their lives has always

been a priority. Still, I haven't always been adept at navigating those discussions with due attention to the needs of all my students. When addressing issues surrounding traumas students may have faced, our number one priority as teachers must be responsiveness to student needs. The following is a brief narrative of how my practices regarding the discussion of race and racism in my class have shifted to be more responsive to the traumas my students of color face.

A decade ago, as a young, enthusiastic teacher with a good foundation in ideas surrounding race, I felt confident in navigating discussions of race relevant to our class texts. One year, while outlining topics we would discuss while reading *Othello*, a group of three Black students in my majority-white class groaned, and one called out, "Can we NOT talk about race?" I was prepared for a comment like this coming from a white student. I was ready to gently discuss the necessity of discussions like this, especially in the context of the play we were about to read. However, I was unprepared for this response from a Black student. The student elaborated, speaking of how he and his Black friends in the class had to deal with race every day and didn't want to deal with it in the classroom.

I will forever be grateful to those students for putting me, a well-meaning white lady, in my place. These students had no reason to trust me to handle this complex subject. They had no reason to believe that class discussion wouldn't inflict more harm than good, potentially causing additional trauma or retraumatization. My shock at their response revealed my blind spots and a single story about what was helpful and meaningful to those outside my own experience. At that moment, I realized the hypocrisy of continuing to teach about racism to contribute to my vision of a more just society while actively harming those in front of me. We continued to discuss social class and gender in *Othello*, but we omitted discussions of race. I felt this was essential to respect these students' wishes.

The following year, I knew I needed a new approach. It still felt important to me to have these conversations. My white students needed to explore such issues they were often able to ignore, and my students of color needed to see themselves in the curriculum and receive validation for their experiences. However, this could not take place at the expense of their comfort in my classroom. I took three approaches to navigate these conversations while respecting the possible trauma of my students of color: ask, frontload, and don't overlook joy.

Ask. Before beginning a unit where race may be a central topic of discussion, I inform my students of the content and describe the incident with my former students. I let them know that I recognize my ability to walk away from discussions about race when I want, but not all people have that privilege. I told them that if anyone doesn't want to discuss this for that reason, we won't. It is communicated to everyone in the class, so I am not assuming the identity of any member of my class, and everyone receives the message loud and clear that I value them and their lived experiences. This is a statement made to the whole class when I have multiple students of color in class. When there is only one student who is a student of color, this is done via email to prevent unwanted attention directed toward a single student.

Frontload. When we engage in these discussions, I frontload some information on terminology and approaches to help set the tone. For instance, when discussing dated texts, we come across dated terms such as "Negro" or "Colored." I explain to my students that, unless we are quoting, we will not use those dated, harmful, and inappropriate terms. I explain which terms are appropriate to use, which terms are okay to quote, and which words are never okay, even in a quote. We also talk about having a safe space to grow, that we will all approach each other with the benefit of the doubt, and that I may correct or question some assumptions, but it's all for us to grow together, not to call one another out. I become vulnerable by giving examples of my growth on many issues to support this. Beyond sharing the example of when my students asked not to talk about race, which exposed my limited knowledge, I also shared with students how, for several years, I rejected anything that was too "girly." I would dress in only dark colors and refuse to enjoy music by artists like Taylor Swift because I had internalized the idea that things girls enjoyed were frivolous and displayed a lack of intelligence. It was only in realizing my internalized sexism that I became free to be a Swiftie who enjoys flowers and the color pink. I explained that my sexism didn't just hurt me but also my interactions with girls and women around me.

Don't overlook joy. Finally, race must be not only discussed in my class as an issue connected to trauma. Texts written by and featuring people of color that are not primarily about racism are essential, as are texts that specifically address this tension, as discussed in Chapter 3. I have several examples of units I take care to feature, specifically Black joy, but one example is a novel study of *Their Eyes Were Watching God* by Zora Neale Hurston. In this unit, we discuss representation, how representation can be a burden, and the importance of representing joy. In addition to the novel, texts used in this unit include "*The Danger of a Single Story*" by Chimamanda Ngozi Adichie, "*Black Boys Play the Classics*" by Toi Derricotte, "*Formation*" by Beyoncé Knowles-Carter, "*There are Birds Here*" by Jamaal May, "*What Does the Academy Value in Black Performance?*" by

> Brandon K. Thorp, and "*Between Laughter and Tears*" by Richard Wright. These texts bridge periods and genres to discuss representation and give students multiple access points.
>
> Since I have put these practices in place, students have yet to ask to avoid the topic of race in discussions. Some students of color have come up to me to speak of how it feels to have conversations about race in the classroom—how they feel singled out or like everyone turns to them, about how they must do the work of teaching everyone else. As we have this conversation, they say it's hard, but they still want to engage in the work, and they appreciate that I gave them an out if they wanted and put in the work to do it right. For these students, being empowered with the choice of engaging in this work and seeing themselves represented in multiple ways makes all the difference.
>
> Each year, in each class, I learn a bit more from my students about how to best make space for them, primarily by valuing their voice and choice. There is no way for a teacher to know every way a student may react to class topics, but we can always work toward creating an environment where students feel comfortable letting us know what they need and adjusting as we go. I must accept that I do not know everything and will need to learn, adapt, revise, and grow continuously. There isn't a silver bullet for ensuring that these discussions won't cause trauma, but having a plan is crucial to knowing what I can do now and how to change my instructional practices.

We are grateful to Dr. Bianchi-Pennington for her willingness to share this challenging and complex moment. As we bore witness, we remembered that we are not perfect, and we are, or should be, constantly learning and evolving our practices and instruction to avoid causing harm (Parker, 2022). Moreover, we remember that while the stories we use may be about past traumatic experiences, such as racist acts, it is necessary to examine what this looks like in today's time, too, addressing issues and realities of students' experiences and that of their communities.

Trigger Warnings

Unfortunately, while we understand the power of critical dialogue and stories—through shared narratives and personal accounts or by reading stories of others—we cannot prepare for every comment or experience our students face. We want to consider how students may get retraumatized from talking about personal situations or listening to others' experiences. Many educators worry about bringing up what could be a scary situation—but we must not shy away. Instead, we should embed this learning in developmentally appropriate ways and consider how the opportunity to process and reprocess traumatic experiences can facilitate healthy coping (Perry, 2014, p. 5). We must keep in mind and consider possible student responses and how they will need resources to weigh options and learn more (Fisher et al., 2020). We must also be aware that some topics and students' comments may inadvertently trigger memories or reactions. We must thus remind everyone that if a student expresses extreme sadness or issues during or after conversations through social interaction or academic performance, it is essential to reach out to licensed school officials. This leads us to a discussion of trigger warnings.

Trigger warnings often indicate when content or spaces are not "safe," potentially leading to adverse traumatic and emotional experiences. Trigger warnings are intended to empower individuals to psychologically prepare for or avoid this content or situations that cause distress. In the classroom, a trigger warning is a practice of "teachers offering prior notification of an educational topic so that students may prepare for or avoid the distress that is automatically evoked by that topic due to clinical mental health problems" (Boysen, 2017, p. 164). However, some believe that trigger warnings can cause harm or are not meaningful (Sanson et al., 2019) because they shelter students by removing any material or discussion that may cause discomfort or stress (Lukianoff & Haidt, 2015). By doing so, trigger warnings undermine students' preparation for the "real world" or misrepresent trauma survivors as unable to encounter complex content in life (Bellet et al., 2020).

We must choose texts and design instruction considering children's developmental levels, especially their emotional and psychological lives. We recommend talking with students about the upcoming material and activities and sharing that some of the material may be sensitive or cause distress, especially for those experiencing traumatic experiences in their personal lives. Teachers must consider students' feelings and the potential for retraumatization when it comes to the content and themes of a chosen novel. We recommend reaching out to the school counselor and others knowledgeable about the novel's content. These people may come to speak to your class, offer coping strategies, provide resources, or share ways to respond to a student who has been triggered during classroom activities. You and the students must know where to go to seek additional support. We also recommend having an alternative novel or backup activities for any student who expresses a desire to opt out of the chosen novel or when students appear uncomfortable with the direction of the discussion.

Restorative Practices and Circles

Importantly, as educators, we often get frustrated with students when they do not handle difficult conversations well or act impulsively when they disagree. You may remember a student you had removed from your room for disrupting another student or not agreeing with your perspective. These are important because hot moments are difficult to maneuver around and through at the moment. For these reasons, we want to briefly mention restorative justice's power. Restorative justice practices, philosophy, principles, and guidance are worldwide, some stemming from ancient and Indigenous ways of being (Winn et al., 2021). This approach centers on social engagement instead of control and power (Morrison, 2012). Restorative justice can be used as a preventative measure, as part of building classroom and school community, and as an intervention when harm has occurred in the classroom or across the school community.

Investigating a restorative approach is vital for trauma-sensitive schools that prioritize students' emotions and experiences within classrooms, as these practices are fundamental in supporting, encouraging, modeling appropriate behaviors, and developing peer relationships. Doing so is vital because students experiencing trauma need systems and protocols to move past their anxiety and fear to make better decisions and build strong relationships (Fisher et al., 2020; O'Drobinak & Kelley, 2021). Restorative practices are an alternative to traditional discipline procedures (Smith et al., 2015). They provide opportunities to explore deeper into disruptive or misunderstood behavior to understand what is prompting the action and words, and when it occurs, to see if there are environmental or school-related factors to consider. In other words, it isn't a "rule" that gets broken versus a relationship that may have been violated and needs to be discussed and addressed—together—because restorative practices offer a framework for repairing peer relationships (Fisher et al., 2020).

Notably, students who are in conflict have difficulty resolving issues without a system. Restorative conferences may be an avenue to move forward when harm occurs, but it is only possible if the victim(s) and perpetrator(s) agree to this option (Fisher et al., 2020). Family members or friends may be invited to the conference, depending on the circumstances. Costello and colleagues (2009) provide a helpful questioning protocol that poses the following questions to the person affected or harmed by the challenging behavior:

- What did you think about when you realized what happened?
- What impact has this had on you and others?
- What has been the hardest thing for you?
- What do you think needs to happen to make things right? (p. 16)

The child who has exhibited the challenging behavior is asked:

- What happened?
- What were you thinking about at the time?
- What have you thought about since?

- Who has been affected by what you have done? In what ways have they been affected?
- What do you think you might need to do to make things right? (p. 16)

The facilitator then engages those present and asks the victim what they would like to see as an outcome of the conference. The perpetrator is asked how they would like to make amends, and when an agreement is reached, a contract is created between the two parties. It is important to note that holding restorative conferences does not imply that disciplinary actions are also needed, as both may be used together. We highly recommend *Restorative Justice in the English Language Arts Classroom* by Winn and colleagues (2021) for more information on this approach as they discuss community-building and other types of circles for beginning restorative conversations specific to an ELA classroom. Other books we recommend reading to learn more about restorative practices include the following:

- *Better Than Carrots or Sticks: Restorative Practices for Positive Classroom Management* by D. Smith, D. Fisher, and N. Frey.
- *Circle Forward: Building a Restorative School Community* by C. Boyes-Watson, K. Pranis, and N. Riestenberg.
- *Implementing Restorative Practices in Schools: A Practical Guide to Transforming School Communities* by M. Thorsborne.
- *Restorative Justice in Education: Transforming Teaching and Learning through the Disciplines* edited by M. T. Winn and L. T. Winn.
- *Using Restorative Circles in Schools* by N. Wroldsen.

MANDATED REPORTING

As teachers, we are not trauma-informed counselors; we are not trained to help students deal with mental health crises or other fallouts from traumatic events. However, we want to build trust relationships with our students. As educators, we spend excessive time with English teachers. Overwhelmingly, we find them to be wise, insightful, brilliant, and dedicated human beings who care deeply about their students, disciplines, and craft. Because you are reading this book in your nonexistent spare time, we know you share these characteristics, and we know that your expertise in pedagogy and ELA is invaluable. Remember, though, that counseling programs require double the education and triple the field experience of teacher education programs. We English teachers have invaluable expertise—but not in this area.

We are not therapists and should not attempt to fill that role. Our role, ultimately, is to refer students to those with the expertise they need.

Therefore, although we have many responsibilities when students verbally share or write about their trauma, diagnosing it is not one of them. It is complicated and unnecessary for teachers to diagnose trauma, which is not our role (Day, 2019). Instead, we must understand common responses to trauma so we can build "awareness of trauma's impacts on learners and the learning space, as well as [the] ability to interpret even disruptive student behaviors as learned coping mechanisms rather than simply personal weaknesses" (Day, 2019, p. 152). In other words, we must understand that students may act in ways that have nothing to do with our classroom instruction or learning. By welcoming our students' voices and inviting students' curiosities and lived experiences into our classrooms, we can learn not to blame a student for a lack of engagement. Instead, we can work to understand what is wrong and how we can help. And while this book does not go into restorative practices, we share below a brief description of what these practices are and why we recommend embedding them alongside trauma-sensitive literacy instruction.

One essential aspect of engaging in TSLI that we must take a moment to discuss is that while we build relationships with our students and want them to feel safe and welcomed in our classrooms, we also need to ensure that all students understand that what they share may or may not be confidential. We owe them honesty, so we should be upfront from the beginning of the year and explain that there are laws governing what we, as teachers, are required to report and to whom. In nearly every state in the United States, teachers are mandated reporters, and students need to be aware of this. Specific definitions of mandated reporters—and, importantly, of the point at which mandated reporters are required to report—differ across states (Child Welfare Information Gateway, 2019). However, in most cases, teachers are required by law to report suspicion of child abuse or neglect. The state of South Carolina, where Britnie lives and Rachelle used to live, puts it this way: "Mandated reporters must report suspected child abuse or neglect when, in their professional capacity, they receive information giving them reason to believe that a child's physical or mental health or welfare has been or may be adversely affected by abuse or neglect" (Children's Law Center, 2018, p. 2).

You've already spent ample time reading this book; now please take an extra few minutes to ensure you understand the expectations of mandated reporters in your state. We've provided a QR code to a helpful guide here but be aware that these laws change often. The guide we refer to here is published by the Children's Bureau division of the U.S. Department of Health and Human Services.

If you invite students to share, discuss, and write about trauma, they must know ahead of time that you are a mandated reporter. In other words, they need to know that you have a legal obligation to report child abuse or neglect. Trust can be violated if students assume that what they write about

Figure 7.1. ***Mandatory Reporters of Child Abuse and Neglect*****: A Factsheet from the Children's Bureau, a Division of the U. S. Department of Health and Human Services**

Source: Child Welfare Information Gateway. (2019). Mandatory Reporters of Child Abuse and Neglect. Washington, DC: U.S. Department of Health and Human Services, Children's Bureau.

is private when—if it meets your state's definition of reasonable suspicion of child abuse or neglect—the reality is that you, as an educator, must report it. Therefore, it is necessary to know the school, district, and state requirements for reporting incidents and to be upfront with students about what you must report before engaging in difficult discussions. If a student shares alarming information, talk with the student and then decide the next steps together. It is essential not to make hasty assumptions, so take the time to gather information and learn more about the situation (Fisher et al., 2020).

THE EMOTIONAL LABOR OF TEACHING, COMPASSION FATIGUE, AND COMPASSION SATISFACTION

As we all know, teaching is emotionally fraught work. By now, many of us have probably heard the term "emotional labor," or the "effort, planning and control needed to express organizationally desired emotions during interpersonal transactions" (Kariou et al., 2021, p. 1). Initially, this term described workers in the service industry, where it was assumed that workers must perform particular emotions—such as openness, patience, and cheerfulness—to be considered professionally competent. In 1983, Arlie Hochschild was the first to study teachers' emotional labor. Since then, scholars have noted that teachers have particularly high expectations related to emotional labor:

> Teachers are constantly exposed to the criticism of their students, parents, coworkers and principals, and are forced to deal with numerous emotional situations and at the same time be a role model for their students . . . they need to

> manage their own anger in the classroom, show sympathy for awkward situations, show care for the progress of their students, continuously encourage them and their parents, and collaborate with their colleagues. Finally, problematic behaviors are more frequent in schools compared with other work environments. (Kariou et al., 2021, p. 2)

In other words, teachers' emotional labor is more complex than that required of workers in other service sectors because teachers are not only "aligning with prescribed emotional-display rules" but because competent handling of our emotions is necessary if we are to help students reach learning goals (p. 2). As Kaplan (2019), writing for Edutopia, put it: emotional labor in teaching is "work that is often invisible and almost always undercompensated—and it's also really, really hard" (n.p.). At times, this can lead to depression and anxiety, prompting us to hold back our feelings and experiences as we teach (Noddings, 2012, 2013).

Scholars have agreed that what counts as professionally acceptable emotional work in teaching is generally defined only implicitly (Winograd, 2003; Zembylas, 2005). Nonetheless, it often involves showing love, or at least enthusiasm, for students; having a passion for the subject matter taught; avoiding emotional extremes; and evincing love for the job itself (Winograd, 2003). While the specific "emotion rules" of teaching may vary, scholars continue to note that teaching is increasingly being treated as a service industry where students and parents are the consumers (Hochschild, 1983; Kariou et al., 2021; Tsang, 2011). As this happens, teachers are expected to perform more and more emotional labor.

Of course, given that trauma-sensitive literacy instruction explicitly asks us all to allow greater space for emotions in our classrooms, we may assume that supporting students who experience trauma may lead to a more significant—perhaps unmanageable—need for emotional labor. This is a valid concern, and one we should explore. Indeed, a recent review of the literature on emotional labor and teaching highlights a correlation between emotional labor and burnout (Kariou et al., 2021). However, by digging deeper into the types of emotional labor that scholars have identified, something fascinating emerges: Emotional labor may not always lead to burnout.

Three types of emotional labor are identified in research: surface acting, deep acting, and—most recently—naturally felt emotions (Hochschild, 1983; Kariou et al., 2021). Surface acting happens when we feel the need to act as if we feel a certain, professionally acceptable way when we don't. Deep acting happens when we strive to feel the way our profession deems acceptable, and "naturally felt emotions" is a label for how we actually feel. For example, in some situations, we might feel a sense of empathy for our students, and we convey that (naturally felt emotions). At other times, we might feel that we should, as professionals, feel a sense of empathy for our students, so we strive to feel that way (deep acting). In other situations, however, we might know that it's important that we appear empathetic to a given student, but we can't get there. However, we act that way because it is a professional expectation of the job. This last one is an example of surface acting, and—perhaps unsurprisingly—it's the type of emotional labor most correlated with burnout.

This means the other two types of emotional labor—deep acting and naturally felt emotions—may not necessarily harm our well-being. Instead, many emotions that are professionally expected of teachers are healthy and positive: empathy, excitement, happiness, patience, trust, engagement, fascination, amusement, bemusement, pride, joy, and so on. There's a reason this job is better than cubicle jobs, right? Right. Fascinatingly, the research is beginning to uncover this. In one of the greatest academic sentences of all time, Kariou and colleagues (2021) note the following: "We should not forget the fact that teaching can also be a source of positive emotions" (p. 10). Exactly. Kariou and colleagues (2021) cite multiple studies to conclude that "naturally felt emotions and deep acting" can moderate or "buffer the negative effects of burnout" (p. 10).

Put more simply: When we actually feel the positive emotions that teaching expects, we are less likely to burn out. Perhaps trauma-sensitive literacy instruction might buffer us from burnout because we can feel—and act upon—our sense of empathy and care for students. As Kariou and colleagues (2021) point out, more research is certainly needed in this area. Nonetheless, these findings echo those from an earlier review of emotional labor and teaching published over a decade ago (Tsang, 2011). In that article, 13 of the 19 studies reviewed found that "performing emotional labor may enhance teachers' job commitment, satisfaction, excitement, self-fulfillment, and professional identity" (p. 1314).

It's nice to hear good news every so often, isn't it? Each of us must remember that the "risk and stakes for sharing hurt are not equal, and sometimes doing emotion work can be a protective act" (Dunn, 2021, p. 149). As educators, we want to consistently check in on ourselves and our needs (Elliott et al., 2018; Romero et al., 2018). Let's read Steven Jernigan's thoughts, a high school ELA teacher, as he shares with us how he maneuvers through the stress of teaching and engaging in the important work of TSLI.

> I start each of my classes with a mindfulness moment. Their contents vary—some days we begin with a 1-minute meditation, while other days we watch videos about how people take pictures of the sunrise to incorporate mindfulness into their morning—but they all have the same purpose. We are taking this short moment before class to give ourselves a second to refocus and become present—to set up our minds to tackle the tasks we have in front of us. Additionally, I tell my students that taking these moments to ground ourselves does not negate, solve, or take away

any of the baggage we bring into the classroom. Still, it can give us some tools to handle it, see it in a different light, or work with it.

And when I think about what self-care in this profession and for myself—or any aspect of our lives—actually means, I think about that last point that I tell my students. Taking breaks or setting boundaries does not negate, solve, or take away the things that plague education. Instead, these actions can give us some methods and tools to be more present for our students, avoid the burnout consuming so many of us, and hopefully put in what this job requires of us without losing ourselves entirely.

When it comes to my self-care, I first and foremost tend to fall back on some advice a professor gave me as an undergrad: set a boundary on the amount of time you will work outside of your contract hours—be it grading papers and planning lessons, or emotionally. The reality is that we as teachers must work outside of our contract hours and during our own time at one point or another. It's exploitative and disrespectful to my personal life outside of the classroom. However, until there is some radical shift in how we think about work/life boundaries and how we have decided to rely on personal sacrifice to maintain our current education system, this expectation of always being "at work" in some way will be the existing reality. Hence the importance of setting specific boundaries of what time you are willing to give up. I have to balance my teaching duties and my desire to enjoy life—and I have to provide the time to walk away.

Another way I cope with education stressors—restrictive laws, underwhelming budgets, a piling of responsibilities, neglected children, and so on—is by having a community of teachers I can turn to. It is essential to talk, dissect, and break down what we are all going through and doing and how we are supporting or hurting with and for our students. This suggestion does not mean forming a cohort at your school whose sole purpose is complaining but instead finding a group of people who understand your tiredness and speak the same language regarding workplace issues and solutions. This work is hard, and going it alone makes it that much harder; in an individualistic society, community care and support are profoundly radical acts of love and rebellion. Having a community separate from teaching is just as important. For me, the ability to step away and fully be someone different than your teacher self is a healing act and a rejuvenating one.

Finally, and perhaps most importantly, I make space for joy both in my work and personal life. For the classroom, this looks like being vulnerable. Namely, I am open and honest with my students. This decision is perhaps borne out of my specific life events, but for me, it is paramount to my sustained existence as a teacher. For example, teaching often requires us to be "on" even when we don't always want to be. Being vulnerable then allows me to explain to my students when I need a little more grace from them that day or admit that I have made a mistake in the lesson or even that I don't know that grammar rule and I need to look it up. It allows me to be human, which is liberating. If I am being honest, it is also wildly frustrating as my need and desire to be seen as a person often comes into focus through a system that often asks me to compartmentalize. Once, I remember a teacher coming to work after her father had died. Her father was older, and while many felt like the teacher should have seen it coming, it was still a moment of grief she felt forced to share with students—it's often easier to simply go to work rather than make the necessary plans to take a day off. In writing this, I am also reminded of the teacher who addressed his class after a student died or another teacher who broke down at lunch because she felt conflicted about taking days off to see their sick mother. I think of the stress I felt when being asked to go to work as COVID cases kept climbing or when I felt it easier to go to work over taking a day to deal with my loss. Again, being open, honest, and vulnerable to my students in these moments is both frankly annoying and a way to maintain who I am.

However, it is essential to acknowledge that highlighting my vulnerability while in the classroom does not equate to trauma dumping on my students sans consequences. I keep and establish appropriate boundaries and am not treating my students like my therapist. I do this by establishing a culture of vulnerability amongst my students and honoring the humanity students and teachers bring into the classroom. In addressing those points, I must admit I have it easy. In the ELA classroom, we have the luxury of diving into works that ooze emotion. Therefore, replication, analysis, and discussion require us to contend with the author's emotions, ourselves, and the characters within the story. "Why did you choose that quote from the story," "what shows you the characters feel this way," and "What message is the author trying to convey" are all questions that saturate my classroom.

Additionally, I make time for community building in my room, not just the icebreakers that make up week 1 lesson plans. Instead, I create games, lessons, and situations that require collaboration—before you counter by questioning whether you have time for this, I promise you that one Friday a quarter of an hour or 5 to 10 minutes once a week is worth it. This should not derail your year-long goals. The purpose is that when students reach a moment where they need or feel compelled to share, they are doing so in a community rather than a classroom. How does that then relate to me being vulnerable? Simply put, I get to model the language around what it means to be exposed or share something difficult. In addressing the COVID scenarios, I remember just naming for my students that even if they didn't need the mindfulness moments we were taking, I needed them because I was worried. I remember sharing poems and things I was reading with my students as they related to my grief. From day one, I had honestly established and fit with our classroom culture.

For my home, this looks like taking advantage of the boundaries I set around my time. Whether taking a walk to ground myself and decompress, eating dinner with my wife, or sinking into a show/movie/game, I aim to try and fill the time I give myself with something that makes me happy. And if the day is hard, sometimes the thing that makes me happy is going to bed at 8:45. I know that while I care about my students and want to ensure all are okay, I must step away. Compassion fatigue is real. As I write this out, though, I want to acknowledge that these moments of joy I create for myself are a privilege that not everyone in teaching has, specifically not everyone who works. I imagine it can be infuriating to hear "make space for joy in your free time" when you cannot have free time because of economic, physical, or emotional hardships. There is no balm for that that I can offer in this specific space. My only response is to find a community and care for one another.

On a lighter note, however, I would like to recall one final piece of advice from that same undergraduate professor: Whenever you grade papers, do so while drinking white wine; it doesn't stain as quickly as red.

Compassion Fatigue and Secondary Traumatic Stress

By pointing out the potential benefits of the emotional side of teaching, we in no way want to contribute to "toxic positivity," which expects that teachers act as though all is well regardless of the circumstances. Instead, teachers are at risk for secondary traumatic stress and compassion fatigue (Ormiston et al., 2022). One survey, for example, found that 43% of teachers demonstrated symptoms of secondary traumatic stress (Koenig et al., 2017). A recent review agrees that teachers are at risk for compassion fatigue and secondary traumatic stress (Ormiston et al., 2022). However, the review also notes that this research is still in its infancy, so we have much to learn.

Ormiston and her colleagues (2022) argue that one thing we must learn is the difference between secondary traumatic stress and compassion fatigue. They define secondary traumatic stress as "oversensitivity to trauma-related stimuli and negatively impacted daily functioning" given "exposure to a student's trauma (current or historical) and a desire to help the student"

(p. 12). This vicarious trauma can lead to the same symptoms as any other trauma—cognitive issues, depression, fatigue, substance abuse, and much more. These secondary effects of exposure to trauma can leave caring educators with a "lowered tolerance for frustration, an aversion to working with certain students, and decreased job satisfaction" (Elliott et al., 2018, p. 29)—in other words, secondary traumatic stress can lead to compassion fatigue, which is chronic.

Compassion fatigue is a "reduced empathic capacity from being exposed to students' experiences (including student trauma histories) and a reduced sense of self-efficacy to respond to the trauma (due to multiple exposures or because of inadequate personal and/or systemic resources) that can reduce a teacher's job satisfaction and performance" (Ormiston et al., 2022, p. 12). Although neither secondary traumatic stress nor compassion fatigue in teachers is well studied, it seems that compassion fatigue is more common in underserved schools and schools with higher proportions of racially, ethnically, or economically marginalized students (Abraham-Cook, 2012; Christian-Brandt et al., 2020; Denham, 2018). In addition, early studies suggest that some teachers are at greater risk for compassion fatigue or secondary traumatic stress than others: "[I]t is important to especially monitor special education teachers, teachers working with students from low socioeconomic backgrounds, and teachers who have experienced trauma themselves" (Ormiston et al., 2022, p. 14).

From Compassion Fatigue to Compassion Satisfaction

Ormiston and colleagues (2022) point out that compassion fatigue has a corollary: compassion satisfaction. Just as *virtuous cycles* serve as the less well-known opposite of *vicious cycles*, compassion satisfaction complements compassion fatigue. The million-dollar question is: How do we get to compassion satisfaction? Again, this body of research is in its infancy, but Ormiston and her colleagues' (2022) review of currently available studies reveal the following:

- Learning more about trauma—and trauma-sensitive and/or trauma-informed instruction—appears to reduce the impact of compassion fatigue for some teachers (Ormiston et al., 2022). Craig (2017) notes that learning about trauma, its impact on students, the awareness of compassion fatigue, and action steps for addressing it can be protective factors for adults. Such learning can also reduce teachers' desire to leave the profession (Peterson, 2019).
- Maintaining a healthy work–life balance can reduce compassion fatigue (Ormiston, 2022). We know you've heard this one before. We all have. If you are interested in hearing from two highly compassionate authors on the subject, we recommend two books:

    - *Onward: Cultivating Emotional Resilience in Educators*, by Elena Aguilar
    - *The Happy Teacher Habits: 11 Habits of the Happiest, Most Effective Teachers on Earth*, by Michael Linsin
- Developing a solid social support network has been shown to reduce teachers' reports of secondary traumatic stress (Abraham-Cook, 2012), and engaging in collaborative "reflective supervision" can support teachers in getting compassion satisfaction (Brown, 2016; Lepore, 2016). In reflective supervision, teachers share emotional reactions to students' experiences with supportive peers and colleagues, which can improve teachers' self-efficacy and compassion satisfaction (Brown, 2016).
- Finally, learning to care for ourselves is essential. If we do not continuously check in on ourselves, we risk feeling ineffective, experiencing compassion fatigue, and inadvertently having lowered tolerance for some students (Elliott et al., 2018). The Lesley Center for Special Education Institute for Trauma Sensitivity recommends boundary setting and mindfulness; we must "identify what is in [our] control and what is not and be fully present at the task at hand," learn when to say no, and engage daily in what brings us joy.

As Arlie Hochschild said in a recent interview, "what makes emotional labor gratifying rather than burdensome is a functioning care system" (Kaplan, 2019, n.p.). In her view, teachers have become the "shock absorbers" for an overburdened educational system and are not equipped to take care of students as entire people. To support teachers emotionally, teachers need to work in environments where their voices are valued and respected and to feel that they are part of a larger team. As Kaplan (2019) noted, the system is healthy "when teachers can shoulder a normal, appropriate range of emotional stress—but are not expected to take responsibility for the ills of society" (n.p.). Therefore, we must consider ways to collaborate with peers at school.

Reaching Out to Others at School

As Steven shared earlier, he seeks community and mindfulness. We must have a community to support our self-care. Importantly, space for these should be present at the school, too, so that teachers and students have a place to go during school hours if they need to step away for a few minutes to "restore their energy" (Fisher et al., 2020, p. 112). We want school administration, staff, and school counselors to know our work and why it is important to us. By sharing at the start of the year that you want to invite students' voices and experiences into your classroom and by asking for resources and support, you will gather a wealth of additional information, ideas, and next steps from your school community. Many school counselors can provide resources not mentioned in this book that can connect with your topics and unit themes. They may want to guest-speak in your class or to reach out to someone in the community to come and share their expertise. It is crucial to have this open communication because, as educators, we are one person. As noted in Mrs. McGee's example, she viewed the school principal as a resource for her students, and so did they.

Through conversations at home, with other teachers and peers, and with community members, students can collaboratively grapple with their feelings, whether they are a response to situations presented in books, real-world events, or their writing, to enhance their awareness of their relationships and circumstances. Community and family members may have experiences connected to classroom discussions and learning, so they bring their firsthand experience and knowledge to share and allow students to learn from them. Additionally, mental health providers and services could support specific recommendations about teachers' triggers and student coping mechanisms, along with the benefit of students learning about mental health services (Craig, 2017). Importantly, family and community representation provide the chance to extend trauma-sensitive literacy instruction efforts beyond the classroom and schoolyard gate. After all, "families are children's first teachers, and community members are critical for advising on the culturally sustaining focus of the initiative" (Fisher et al., 2020, p. 106). Instead of "adopting an approach that is a one-way transmission model that relies on telling parents how to improve," we can "come from a place of respecting and working with families' perspectives and contributions" (p. 111).

Right now, you may be wondering how to get your administration on board. This is a great question, especially when most trauma-sensitive school research emphasizes a whole-school approach. There is a need for micro- and macro-level support when implementing trauma-sensitive practices, and no single approach can effectively minimize harm or guarantee student resilience (Everett, 2021). The micro-level may include the skills and strategies discussed in our book at the individual teacher level.

The macro-level supports are schoolwide and often at the programmatic level. The Trauma-Sensitive School Checklist, developed by Lesley University in partnership with TLPI, provides a checklist of questions organized by five components needed to create a trauma-sensitive school: schoolwide policies and practices, classroom strategies and techniques, collaborations and linkages with mental health, family partnerships, and community linkages. School leadership teams should consider their linkages to mental health services, the extent of their family partnerships, and ties to community agencies. The work is extensive, and the intent is not to suggest that all these categories must be addressed simultaneously. Instead, the checklist results give teams a decision-making mechanism for determining where efforts need to be focused and in what order.

We also recommend viewing the information and resources provided by the Trauma and Learning Policy Initiative with your school administration. Its website shares six attributes of trauma-sensitive schools, as well as tools and resources for creating them; discusses why we need them; and shows how schools can be trauma sensitive (traumasensitiveschools.org). The website also provides access to research and "how-to" guides, such as the one titled, *Helping Traumatized Children Learn, Vol. 2: Creating and Advocating for Trauma-Sensitive Schools*. Additional ideas provided by Lesley's Center for Special Education's Institute for Trauma Sensitivity are the following:

1. Know what is yours to do: Identify what is in your control and what is not and be fully present at the task at hand.
2. Let go of the result: Realize that what we think should be may not be the best idea.
3. Develop a self-care strategy to take care of yourself: Discover what brings you joy, engage in it daily, and learn how and when to say no.
4. Create a strong network: Build your community of allies.
5. Be authentic: Be honest with yourself and others, including your students, about who you are.
6. Practice mindfulness: Accept what is currently happening—be present. (n.p.)

CONCLUSION

In the meantime, we must find ways to care for ourselves and our colleagues. Find joy in something you love outside of work. Build a support system. And rest well knowing that you have indeed, by reading this book, armed yourself with knowledge about trauma-sensitive literacy instruction. We hope you find this book helpful as you traverse both the fatigue and satisfaction that make teaching among the best of jobs, and we look forward to the years ahead, in which we will all continue to learn more about how to support students who have experienced trauma.

References

Abolitionist Teaching Network. (2020). *Guide for racial justice & abolitionist social and emotional learning*. ATN.

Abraham-Cook, S. (2012). *The prevalence and correlates of compassion fatigue, compassion satisfaction, and burnout among teachers working in high-poverty urban public schools*. Publication No. 1814. Seton Hall University Dissertations and Theses. ProQuest LLC.

Adichie, C. N. (2009, July). *The danger of a single story*. Ted Talks Video. Retrieved from ted.com/talks/chimamanda_adichie_the_danger_of_a_single_story/up-next?language=en

Afflerbach, P. (2018). *Understanding and using reading assessment: K–12* (3rd ed.). Association for Supervision and Curriculum Development.

Aguilar, E. (2020). *Coaching for equity: Conversations that change practice*. Jossey-Bass.

Aguilar, E. (2018). *Onward: Cultivating emotional resilience in educators*. Jossey-Bass.

Ahmed, S., & Daniels, H. (2017). Identity, empathy, and inquiry: When the world hands us a curriculum. *Literacy Today*, *34*(5), 44–45.

Alim, H. S., & Paris, D. (2017). What is culturally sustaining pedagogy and why does it matter? In D. Paris & H. S. Alim (Eds.), *Culturally sustaining pedagogies: Teaching and learning for justice in a changing world*. Teachers College Press.

Allington, R. L. (2015). What really matters for middle school readers: From research to practice. Pearson.

Allington, R. L., & Gabriel, R. E. (2012). Every child, every day. *Educational Leadership*, *69*(6), 10–15.

Alvarez, A. (2020). Seeing race in the research on youth trauma and education: A critical review. *Review of Educational Research*, *90*(5), 583–626.

American Library Association. (2022). *Challenge reporting*. Ala.org/tools/challengesupport/report

American Library Association. (2022). *Top 10 most challenged books lists*. Ala.org/advocacy/bbooks/frequentlychallengedbooks/top10

Anderson, C. (2000). *How's it going? A practical guide to conferring with student writers*. Heinemann.

Anderson, J. (2019). Hooked on classics. *Harvard Education Journal*, *99*(2), 28–35.

Andolina, M. W., & Conklin, H. G. (2020). Fostering democratic and social-emotional learning in action civics programming: Factors that shape students' learning from project soapbox. *American Educational Research Journal*, *57*(3), 1203–1240.

Applebee, A. N., & Langer, J. A. (2013). *Writing instruction that works: Proven methods for middle and high school classrooms*. Teachers College Press.

Atwell, N. (2015). In the middle: A lifetime of learning about writing, reading, and adolescents (3rd ed.). Heinemann.

Aukerman, M. (2013). Rereading comprehension pedagogies: Toward a dialogic teaching ethic that honors student sensemaking. *Dialogic Pedagogy*, *1*, A1–A31.

Ayers, R., & Ayers, W. (2014). *Teaching the taboo: Courage and imagination in the classroom* (2nd ed.). Teachers College Press.

Bakhtin, M. M. (1984). *Problems of Dostoevsky's poetics*. (C. Emerson, Ed. & Trans.). University of Michigan Press.

Ball, A. (2006). Teaching writing in culturally diverse classrooms. In MacArthur, C. A., Graham, S. & Fitzgerald, J, Eds. *Handbook of writing research* (pp. 293–310). The Guilford Press.

Bandura, A. (1977). *Social learning theory*. Prentice Hall.

Batchelor, K. E. (2018). Using linked text sets to promote advocacy and agency through a critical lens. *Journal of Adolescent & Adult Literacy*, *62*(4), 379–386.

Beach, R., Thein, A. H., & Webb, A. (2016). *Teaching to exceed the English Language Arts Common Core State Standards: A critical inquiry approach for 6–12 classrooms*. (2nd ed.). Routledge.

Beers, K., & Probst, R. E. (2017). *Disrupting thinking: Why how we read matters*. Scholastic.

Bellet, B. W., Jones, P. J., Meyersburg, C. A., Brenneman, M. M., Morehead, K. E., & McNally, R. J. (2020). Trigger warning and resilience in college students: A preregistered replication and extension. *Journal of Experimental Psychology Applied*, *26*(4), 717–723.

Benard, B. (1991). *Fostering resiliency in kids: Protective factors in the family, school, and community*. Western Center for Drug-Free Schools and Communities.

Benard, B. (2004). *Resiliency: What we have learned*. WestEd.

Berman, S. Chaffee, S., & Sarmiento, J. (2018). *The practice base for how we learn: supporting students' social, emotional, and academic development*. The Aspen Institute, National Commission on Social, Emotional, and Academic Dev https://www.aspeninstitute.org/wp-content/uploads/2018/03/CDE-Commission-report.pdf

Bernhard, B. (2022). Students sue Wentzville School District over book banning. STLtoday.com. stltoday.com/news/local/education/students-sue-wentzville-school-district-over-book-banning/article_2979ec1f-1a94-5aae-9057-a9f33f9c2387.html

Bickmore, S. T., & Clark, S. P. (Eds.). (2021). *Expanding the foundation: African American authors of young adult literature, 1980–2000*. Rowman & Littlefield.

Bishop, E. (2014). Critical literacy: Bringing theory to praxis. *Journal of Curriculum Theorizing*, *30*(1), 51–63.

Bonilla-Silva, E. (2014). *Racism without racists: Color-blind racism and the persistence of racial inequality in America* (4th ed.). Rowman & Littlefield Publishers.

Borsheim-Black, C. (2015). "It's pretty much white": Challenges and opportunities of an anti-racist approach to literature instruction in a multi-layered white context. *Research in Teaching of English*, *49*(4), 407–429.

Borsheim-Black, C., Macaluso, M., & Petrone, R. (2014). Critical literature pedagogy: Teaching canonical literature for critical pedagogy. *Journal of Adolescent & Adult Literacy*, *58*(2), 123–133.

Borsheim-Black, C., and Sarigiandes. S.T. (2019). *Letting go of literary whiteness: Anti-racist literature instruction for white students*. Teachers College Press.

Boscolo, P. & Gelati, C. (2019). Motivating writers. In S. Graham, C. MacArthur, & M. Hebert (Eds.), *Best practices in writing instruction* (3rd ed., pp. 51–80). Guilford.

Boston, M. D., & Wilhelm, A. G. (2017). Middle school mathematics instruction in instructionally focused urban districts. *Urban Education*, *52*(7), 829–861.

Boyes-Watson, C., Pranis, K., & Riestenberg, N. (2015). *Circle forward: Building a restorative school community*. Living Justice Press.

Boysen, A. (2017). Evidence-based answers to questions about trigger warnings for clinically-based distress: A review for teachers. *Scholarship of Teaching and Learning in Psychology*, *3*(2), 163–177.

Bransford, J. D., Brown, A. L., & Cocking, R. R. (2000). *How People Learn: Brain, Mind, Experience, and School*. National Academy Press.

Briere, J. N., & Scott, C. (2015). *Principles of trauma therapy: A guide to symptoms, evaluation, and treatment, DSM-5 update* (2nd ed.). Sage.

Brown, B. (2018). *Braving: The Seven elements Of trust*. Dare to Lead. Daretolead .brenebrown.com/wp-content/uploads/2018/10/BRAVING.pdf

Brown, L. (2016). *The impact of reflective supervision on early childhood educators of at-risk children: Fostering compassion satisfaction and reducing burnout*. Publication No. 10193236. Doctoral dissertation, University of California, Santa Barbara. ProQuest LLC.

Bruner, J. (1977). *The process of education: A landmark in educational theory*. Harvard Educational Press.Bryk, A. S., Sebring, P. B., Allensworth, E., Luppescu, S., & Easton, J. Q. (2010). *Organizing schools for improvement: Lessons from Chicago*. University of Chicago Press.

Buehler, J. (2016). *Teaching reading with YA literature*. National Council of Teachers of English.

Calderon, M., & Slakk, S. (2018). *Teaching reading to English language learners, Grades 6–12: A framework for improving achievement in the content areas* (2nd ed.). Guilford.

Carlson, E., Palmieri, P., Field, N., Dalenberg, C., Macia, K., & Spain, D. (2016). Contributions of risk and protective factors to prediction of psychological symptoms after traumatic experiences. *Comprehensive Psychiatry*, *69*, 106–115.

Chambers Cantrell, S., Walker-Dalhouse, D., & Lazar, A. (2022). *Culturally sustaining literacy pedagogies: Honoring students' heritages, literacies, and languages*. Teachers College Press.

Cazden, C. (1988). *Classroom discourse: The language of teaching and learning*. Heinemann.

Chavez, N. (June, 2022). He took his school to the Supreme Court in the 1980s for pulling "objectionable" books. Here's his message to young people. CNN News. Cnn.com/2022/06/25/us/book-bans-island-trees-union-free-school-district -v-pico/index.html

Children's Law Center. (2018). Mandated reporter guide: Understanding your legal duty to report suspected child abuse and neglect. University of South Carolina School of Law. Dss.sc.gov/media/1903/dss-brochure-1955-jan-19.pdf

Child Welfare Information Gateway. (2019). Mandatory reporters of child abuse and neglect. U.S. Department of Health and Human Services: Children's Bureau. childwelfare.gov/pubpdfs/manda.pdf

Christian-Brandt, A. S., Santacrosse, D. E., & Barnett, M. L. (2020). In the trauma-informed care trenches: Teacher compassion satisfaction, secondary traumatic stress, burnout, and intent to leave education within underserved elementary schools. *Child Abuse & Neglect*, *110*(3), 104437. https://doi.org/10.1016/j.chiabu.2020.104437

Cobb, P., Jackson, K., Henrick, E., Smith, T. M., & the MIST team (2018). *Systems for instructional improvement: Creating coherence from the classroom to the district office*. Harvard Education Press.

Cohen, D. K. (2011). *Teaching and its predicaments*. Harvard University Press.

Collaborative for Academic, Social, and Emotional Learning (CASEL). (2003). Safe and sound: An educational leader's guide to evidence-based social and emotional learning (SEL) programs. Published by author. https://casel.org/safe-and-sound-guide-to-sel-programs/

Cole, S. F., Eisner, A., Gregory, M., & Ristuccia, J. (2013). *Helping traumatized children learn: Creating and advocating for trauma-sensitive schools*. Massachusetts Advocates for Children.

Comber, B. (2015). Critical literacy and social justice. *Journal of Adolescent & Adult Literacy*, *58*(5), 362–367.

Cooperative Children's Book Center. (2018). *Books by and/or about Black, Indigenous and people of color*. ccbc.education.wisc.edu/literature-resources/ccbc-diversity-statistics/books-by-and-or-about-poc-2018/#Usonly

Corcoran, C. A., & Mamalakis, A. (2009). Fifth grade students' perceptions of reading motivation techniques. *Reading Improvement*, *46*(3), 137–142.

Costello, B., Wachtel, J., & Wachtel, T. (2009). *The restorative practices handbook: For teachers, disciplinarians and administrators*. International Institute for Restorative Practices.

Cozolino, L. (2014). *The neuroscience of human relationships: Attachment and the developing social brain*. Norton.

Craig, S. E. (2008). *Reaching and teaching children who hurt: Strategies for your classroom*. Brookes Publishing.

Craig, S. E. (2017). *Trauma-sensitive schools for the adolescent years: Promoting resiliency and healing*. Teachers College Press.

Daniels, H. (2002). *Literature circles: Voice and choice in book clubs and reading groups* (2nd ed.). Stenhouse.

Darling-Hammond, L. (2016). Research on teaching and teacher education and its influence on policy and practice. *Educational Researcher*, *45*(2), 83–91.

Day, M. L. (2019). Wounds and writing: Building trauma-informed approaches to writing pedagogy. Electronic Theses and Dissertations. Paper 3178. https://core.ac.uk/download/pdf/223224094.pdf

DeHart, J., Meyer, C., & Walker, K. (Eds.). (2021). *Connecting theory and practice in middle school literacy: Critical conversations*. Routledge.

Delgado, R., & Stefancic, J. (2017). *Critical race theory: An introduction* (3rd ed.). NYU Press.

Demoiny, S. B. (2018). Websites to explore race as a social construct. *Journal of Adolescent & Adult Literacy*, *61*(4), 469–472.

Denham, F. S. (2018). *School building blight and teacher secondary traumatic stress: A quantitative study*. Publication No. 10974259. Doctoral dissertation, Northcentral University. ProQuest LLC.

DiAngelo, R. (2018). *Why it's so hard for white people to talk about racism*. Beacon Press.

Donovan, S. J., & Toliver, S. R. (2019). Story first: Making a movement. *The ALAN Review*, *46*(3) 84–90.

Dunn, M. B. (2021). When teachers hurt: Supporting preservice teacher well-being. *English Education*, *53*(2), 145–151.

Dutro, E. (2010). What "hard times" mean: Mandated curriculum, class-privileged assumptions, and the lives of poor children. *Research in the Teaching of English*, *44*(3), 255–291.

Dutro, E. (2013). Towards a pedagogy of the incomprehensible: Trauma and the imperative of critical witness in literacy classrooms. *Pedagogies: An International Journal*, *8*(4), 301–315.

Dutro, E. (2019). *The vulnerable heart of literacy: Centering trauma as powerful pedagogy*. Teachers College Press.

Dutro, E., & Caasi, E. (2022). The complexities of trauma in responsive teaching. *Language Arts*, *99*(5), 358–362.

Dyches, J., Sams, B., & Boyd, A. S. (Eds.). (2020). *Acts of resistance: Subversive teaching in the English language arts classroom*. Myers Education Press.

Eisenbach, B., & Frydman, J. S. (Eds.). (2021). *Fostering mental health literacy through adolescent literature*. Rowman & Littlefield.

Elliott, K. W., Elliott, J. K., & Spears, S. G. (2018). Teaching on empty. *Principal*, *98*(2), 28–29.

Everett, S. (2021). *Trauma-informed teaching: Cultivating healing-centered ELA classrooms*. National Council of Teachers of English.

Felitti, V. J., Anda, R. F., Nordenberg, D., Williamson, D. F., Spitz, A. M., Edwards, V., . . . Marks, J. S. (1998). Relationship of childhood abuse and household dysfunction to many of the leading causes of death in adults. *American Journal of Preventative Medicine*, *14*(4), 245–258.

Fisher, D., & Frey, N. (2014). *Better learning through structure teaching: A framework for the gradual release of responsibility* (2nd ed.). Association for Supervision and Curriculum Development.

Fisher, D., Frey, N., & Savitz, R. S. (2020). *Teaching hope and resilience for students experiencing trauma: Creating safe and nurturing classrooms for learning*. Teachers College Press.

Flower, L., & Hayes, J. R. (1980). Identifying the organization of writing processes. In L. W. Gregg and E. L. Strindberg (Eds.). *Cognitive processes in writing: An interactive approach* (pp. 3–30). Lawrence Erlbaum.

Freire, P. (1970/2009). *Pedagogy of the oppressed*. (30th anniversary ed.) Continuum.

Frey, N., Fisher, D., & Smith, D. (2019). *All learning is social and emotional: Helping students develop essential skills for the classroom and beyond*. ASCD.

Gallagher, K. (2011). *Write like this: Teaching real-world writing through modeling and mentor texts*. Stenhouse.

Gallo, J., & Herrmann, B. (2018). Shining light in dark corners: Choosing heavy books for the classroom. *English Leadership Quarterly*, *42*(4). Library.ncte.org/journals/ELQ/issues/v42-4/30605

Garcia, A. (2021). Pedagogies of complicity: Perspective taking and healing. *The English Journal*, *111*(1), 21–24.

Gay, G. (2013). Teaching to and through cultural diversity. *Curriculum Inquiry*, *43*(1), 48–70.

Gay, G. (2018). *Culturally responsive teaching: Theory, research, and practice* (3rd ed.). Teachers College Press.

Ginsberg, R., & Glenn, W. J. (Eds.). (2019). *Engaging with multicultural YA literature in the secondary classrooms: Critical approaches to critical education*. Routledge.

Glass, O., Dreusicke, M., Evans, J., Bechard, E., & Wolever, R. Q. (2019). Expressive writing to improve resilience to trauma: A clinical feasibility trial. *Complementary Therapies in Clinical Practice*, *34*, 240–246.

Goldman, S. R., Britt, M. A., Brown, W., Cribb, G., George, M., Greenleaf, C., . . . Project READI. (2016). Disciplinary literacies and learning to read for understanding: A conceptual framework for disciplinary literacy. *Educational Psychologist*, *51*(2), 219–246. Doi.org/10.1080/00461520.2016.1168741

Goldstein, D. (July, 2022). New reading curriculum is mired in debate over race and gender. *The New York Times*. www.nytimes.com/2022/07/21/us/lucy-calkins-race-gender-curriculum.html

Gorski, P. (2020). How trauma-informed are we, really? *Educational Leadership*, *78*(2), 14–19.

Gorski, P. C., & Pothini, S. G. (2018). *Case studies on diversity and social justice education* (2nd ed.). Routledge.

Graham, S. & Harris, K. R. (2019). Evidence-based practices in writing. In Graham, S., MacArthur, C. A. & Hebert, M., Eds. *Best practices in writing instruction* (3rd ed., pp. 3–30). The Guilford Press.

Greathouse, P., & Anthony, H. (Eds.). (2022). *Developing mathematical literacy through adolescent literature*. Rowman & Littlefield.

Greenberg, K. (2022, June 29). Kent school board votes against banning book featuring LGBTQ+ content. K5 News. king5.com/article/news/local/kent-school-board-book-ban-lgbtq-jack-of-hearts-and-other-parts/281-62fb7f12-634c-4cf4-aef1-2e731917e3c5

Gutierrez, K. D., Morales, & Martinez, D. C. (2009). Re-mediating literacy: Culture, difference, and learning for students from nondominant communities. *Review of Research in Education*, *33*(1), 212–245.

Haberl, E. (2019). *The meaningful argument: High stakes argumentative writing and blending genre in a 7th grade classroom*. Unpublished doctoral dissertation. University of Colorado, Boulder.

Hammond, Z. (2015). *Culturally responsive teaching and the brain: Promoting authentic engagement and rigor among culturally and linguistically diverse students*. Corwin.

Harris, E. A., & Alter, A. (2022 April). Book banning efforts surged in 2021. *The New York Times*. nytimes.com/2022/04/04/books/banned-books-libraries.html

Hattie, J. (2012). *Visible learning for teachers: Maximizing impact on learning*. Routledge/Taylor & Francis Group.

Hattie, J. (2018). *Visible learning plus: 250+ influences on student achievement*. us.corwin.com/sites/default/files/250_influences_10.1.2018.pdf

Hattie, J., Stern, J., Fisher, D., & Frey, N. (2020). *Visible learning for social studies: Designing student learning for conceptual understanding*. Corwin.

Hays, A. D. (2021). *Engaging empathy and activating agency: Young adult literature as a catalyst for action*. Rowman & Littlefield.

Helms, J. E. (1990). *Black and White racial identity: Theory, research and practice*. Greenwood Press.

Henderson, N. (2013). Havens of resilience. *Educational Leadership*, *71*(1), 22–27.

Hertel, R., & Johnson, M. M. (2013). How the traumatic experiences of students manifest in school settings. In E. Rossen Jackson & R. Hull (Eds.), *Supporting and educating traumatized students: A guide for school-based professionals* (pp. 23–35). Oxford University Press.

Hillocks, G. (2002). *The testing trap: How state writing assessments control learning*. Teachers College Press.

Hirsh, E. D. (1987). *Cultural literacy*. Vintage Publishing.

Hochschild, A. R. (1983). *The managed heart: Commercialization of human feeling*. University of California Press.

Holmes, M. R., Yoon, S., Berg, K. A., Cage, J. L., & Perzynski, A. T. (2018). Promoting the development of resilient academic functioning in maltreated children. *Child Abuse & Neglect*, *75*, 92–103.

Homrich-Knieling, M. (2019). From rapport to relationships: Shifting our practice from classroom management to community. *Voice from the Middle*, *27*(1), 58–61.

Howard, T. (2017). *Relationships & learning: Keys to academic success*. Teaching Works Working Papers.

International Literacy Association. (2019). *Children's choices* 2019. Literacyworldwide.org/get-resources/reading-lists/childrens-choices-reading-list

Ippolito, J., & Savitz, R. S. (2022). Professional learning should blend SEL and equity: SEL coaches can lead the way. *The Learning Professional*, *43*(2).

Ivey, G., & Johnston, P. (2018). Engaging disturbing books. *Journal of Adolescent & Adult Literacy*, *62*(2), 143–150.

Jackson, K., Wilhelm, A. G., & Munter, C. (2018). Specifying goals for students' mathematics learning and the development of teachers' knowledge, perspectives, and practice. In Cobb, P., Jackson, K., Henrick, E., Smith, T. M., & the MIST team. *Systems for instructional improvement: Creating coherence from the classroom to the district office*. Harvard Education Press.

Jacobs, V. A. (2008). Adolescent literacy: Putting the crisis in context. *Harvard Educational Review*, *78*, 7–39.

Janks, H. (2005). Language and the design of texts. *English Teaching Practice and Critique*, *4*(3), 97–110.

Janks, H. (2010). *Literacy and power*. Taylor & Francis.

Johnson, H., Mathis, J., & Short, K. G. (Eds.). (2017). *Critical content analysis of children's and young adult literature*. Routledge.

Jones, S., Brush, K., Bailey, R., Brion-Meisels, G., McIntyre, J., Kahn, J., Nelson, B., and Stickle, L. (2021). *Navigating SEL from the inside out: Looking inside and across 33 leading SEL programs. A practical resource for schools and OST providers*. The Harvard Graduate School of Education and the Wallace Foundation. www.wallacefoundation.org/knowledge-center/Documents/navigating-social-and-emotional-learning-from-the-inside-out-2ed.pdf

Kane, B. D. (2016). Design conjectures for preservice teachers' concept development about rigorous and equitable writing instruction. *Teaching/Writing: The Journal of Writing Teacher Education*, *5*(1).

Kane, B. D. (2020). Developing professional reasoning in teacher education: Preservice teachers' opportunities for concept development in a practice-based design study. *Teachers College Record*.

Kane, B. D., Morrison, J. D., Aldrich, C., Savitz, R., Ming, K., O'Byrne, W. I., & Lily, T. (2021). Disentangling content-area and disciplinary literacy: A metacognitive approach to professional development. *Literacy Matters*, 21, pp. 77–84.

Kane, B., & Savitz, R. S. (2022). Disciplinary literacy and culturally sustaining pedagogies: Tensions and potential. In S. Chambers Cantrell, D. Walker-Dalhouse, & A. Lazar (Eds.), *Culturally sustaining pedagogy: Developing socially just literacy teaching practices* (pp. 53–74). Teachers College Press.

Kaplan, E. (2019). Teaching your heart out: Emotional labor and the need for systematic change. *Edutopia*. www.edutopia.org/article/teaching-your-heart-out-emotional-labor-and-need-systemic-change

Kariou, A., Koutsimani, P., Montgomery, A., & Lainidi, O. (2021. Emotional labor and burnout among teachers: A systematic review. *International Journal of Environmental Research and Public Health*, *18*(23), 1–15.

Kennedy. M. (1998). *Learning to teach writing: Does teacher education make a difference?* Teachers College Press.

Kinloch, V., Burkhard, T., & Penn, C. (2019). *Race, justice, and activism in literacy instruction*. Teachers College Press.

Kinloch, V., Nemeth, E. A., Butler, T. T., & Player, G. D. (2021). *Where is the justice? Engaged pedagogies in schools and communities*. Teachers College Press.

Koenig, A., Rodger, S., & Specht, J. (2017). Educator burnout and compassion fatigue: A pilot study. *Canadian Journal of School Psychology*, *32*(1), 1–20.

Ladson-Billings, G. (1995). Toward a theory of culturally relevant pedagogy. *American Educational Research Journal*, *32*, 465–491.

Lamott, A. (1994). *Bird by bird: Some instructions on writing and life*. Anchor Books.

Lampert, M., & Graziani, F. (2009). Instructional activities as a tool for teachers' and teacher educators' learning. *The Elementary School Journal*, *109*(5), 491–509.

Lave, J., & Wenger, E. (1991). *Situated learning: Legitimate peripheral participation*. Cambridge University Press.

Lee, C. (2007). *Culture, literacy, and learning: Taking bloom in the midst of the whirlwind*. Teachers College Press.

Lepore, C. E. (2016). *The prevention of preschool teacher stress: Using mixed methods to examine the impact of reflective supervision*. Publication No. 10193227. Doctoral dissertation, University of California, Santa Barbara. ProQuest LLC.

Lesley University. (n.d.). *Six ways for educators to avoid compassion fatigue*. lesley.edu/article/six-ways-for-educators-to-avoid-compassion-fatigue

Leu, D., Forzani, E., Rhoads, C., Maykel, C., Kennedy, C., & Timbrell, N. (2014). The new literacies of online research and comprehension: Rethinking the reading achievement gap. *Reading Research Quarterly*, *50*, 10.1002/rrq.85.

Linsin, M. (2016). *The happy teacher habits: 11 habits of the happiest, most effective teachers on earth.* JME Publishing.

Love, B. (2019). *We want to do more than survive: Abolitionist teaching and the pursuit of educational freedom.* Beacon Press.

Luke, A. (2012). Critical literacy: Foundational notes. *Theory Into Practice, 51,* 4–11.

Lukianoff G., & Haidt J. (September, 2015). The coding of the American mind. *The Atlantic.* theatlantic.com/magazine/archive/2015/09/the-coddling-of-the-american-mind/399356/

Lysaker, J., Tongue, C., Gauson, D., & Miller, A. (2011). Reading and social imagination: What relationally oriented reading instruction can do for children. *Reading Psychology, 32*(6), 520–566.

Malo-Juvera, V., & Greathouse, P. (Eds.). (2020). *Breaking the taboo with young adult literature.* Rowman & Littlefield.

McGee, P. (2017) *Feedback that moves writers forward: How to escape correcting mode to transform student writing.* Corwin Literacy.

McLaughlin, M., & DeVoogd, G. (2004). *Critical literacy: Enhancing students' comprehension of text.* Scholastic.

McLeod, J. D., Uemura, R., & Rohrman, S. (2012). Adolescent mental health, behavior problems, and academic achievement. *Journal of Health and Social Behavior, 53*(4), 482–497.

McTighe, J., & Wiggins, G. (2013). *Essential questions: Opening doors to student understanding.* Association for Supervision and Curriculum Development.

Mattison, A. (2017). *The kite and the string: How to write with spontaneity and control—and live to tell the tale.* Penguin Books.

Meyers, L. (2014). The toll of childhood trauma. *Counseling Today, 57,* 28–36.

Milner, H. R. (2019). Race to improve teacher education: Building awareness for instructional practice. *American Educator, 43*(3), 13–17.

Milner, H. R. (2021). *Start where you are, but don't stay there: Understanding diversity, opportunity gaps, and teaching in today's classrooms* (2nd ed.). Harvard Education Press.

Minor, C. (2018). *We got this: Equity, access, and the quest to be who our students need us to be.* Heinemann.

Mirgain, S. A., & Singles, J. (2016). *Therapeutic Journaling.* va.gov/WHOLEHEALTHLIBRARY/tools/therapeutic-journaling.asp

Mirra, N. (2018). *Educating for empathy: Literacy learning and civic engagement.* Teachers College Press.

Mirra, N., Filipiak, D., & Garcia, A. (2015). Revolutionizing inquiry in urban English classrooms: Pursuing voice and justice through youth participatory action research. *The English Journal, 105*(2), 49–57.

Moje, E. B. (2015). Doing and teaching disciplinary literacy with adolescent learners: A social and cultural enterprise. *Harvard Educational Review, 85*(2), 254–278.

Moll, L. C., Amanti, C., Neff, D., & Gonzalez, N. (1992). Funds of knowledge for teaching: Using a qualitative approach to connect homes and classrooms. *Theory into Practice, 31* (2), 132–141.

Montgomery, D. (January, 2022). Librarians fight back against efforts to ban books in schools. *Education Week.* edweek.org/teaching-learning/librarians-fight-back-against-efforts-to-ban-books-in-schools/2022/01

Morrell, E. (2007). *Critical literacy and urban youth: Pedagogies of access, dissent, and liberation*. Routledge.

Morrell, E. (2008). On Literatures, Literacies, and Liberation. Remarks delivered at the University of Notre Dame. www.academia.edu/37681970/Literatures_Literacies_and_Liberation_1_pdf

Morrison, B. (2012). What is restorative justice? SFU Continuing Studies Series Video. youtube.com/watch?v=sE8TDzlR2tg

Muhammad, G. E. (2020). *Cultivating genius: An equity framework for culturally and historically responsive literacy*. Scholastic.

Munter, C. (2014). Developing visions of high-quality mathematics instruction. *Journal for Research in Mathematics Education*, *45*(5), 584–635.

Natanson, H. (2022, April). More books are banned than ever before, as Congress takes on the issue. *The Washington Post*. washingtonpost.com/education/2022/04/07/book-bans-congress-student-library

National Child Traumatic Stress Network, Justice Consortium, Schools Committee, and Culture Consortium. (2017). *Addressing race and trauma in the classroom: A resource for educators*. National Center for Child Traumatic Stress.

National Coalition Against Censorship. (2020). *The free expression educators handbook*. ncac.org/resource/educator-handbook

National Council of Teachers of English. (2022). Position statement on writing instruction in schools. Published by author. ncte.org/statement/statement-on-writing-instruction-in-school

National Council of Teachers of English (2022). *Intellectual freedom center*. ncte.org/resources/ncte-intellectual-freedom-center

National Governors Association Center for Best Practices & Council of Chief State School Officers. (2010). *Common Core State Standards*. NGACBP & CCSSO.

National Survey of Children's Health. (2019, October). National survey of children's health. mchb.hrsa.gov/sites/default/files/mchb/Data/NSCH/NSCH-2018-factsheet.pdf

National Traumatic Stress Network. (n.d.) *Trauma Types*. nctsn.org/what-is-child-trauma/trauma-types

New York University. (2022). *Culturally responsive curriculum scorecard*. steinhardt.nyu.edu/metrocenter/ejroc/services/culturally-responsive-curriculum-scorecards

Nguyen, T. A. (2018). Cultural competence and literacy: Developing an ethic of care for the 21st-century world. *Literacy Today*, *36*(3), 17–18.

Nieto, S., & Bode, P. (2018). *Affirming diversity: The sociopolitical context of multicultural education* (7th ed.). Pearson.

Noddings, N. (2012). The caring relation in teaching. *Oxford Review of Education*, *38*(6), 771–781.

Noddings, N. (2013). *Caring: A relational approach to ethics and moral education* (2nd. ed.). University of California Press.

Noguera, P. (2019). Cops or counselors? *Teaching when the world is on fire* (Lisa Delpit, Ed.). The New Press.

O'Dougherty Wright, M., Masten, A. S., & Narayan, A. J. (2013). Resilience processes in development: Four waves of research on positive adaptation in the context of adversity. In S. Goldstein & R. B. Brooks (Eds.), *Handbook of resilience in children* (pp. 15–38). Springer.

O'Drobinak, B., & Kelley, B. (2021). *Teaching, learning, and trauma: Responsive practices for holding steady in turbulent times: Grades 6–12*. Corwin.

Ormiston, H. E., Nygaard, M. A., & Apgar, S. (2022). A systematic review of secondary traumatic stress and compassion fatigue in teachers. *School Mental Health*. https://doi.org/10.1007/s12310-022-09525-2

Ortlieb, E., Kane, B. D. & Cheek, E. (in press). *Disciplinary literacies: Unpacking research, theory, and practice*. Guilford Press.

Osher, D., Kendziora, K., Spier, E., & Garibaldi, M. L. (2014). School influences on child and youth development. In D. Z. Sloboda & H. Petras (Eds.), *Advances in Prevention Science Vol. 1: Defining Prevention Science* (pp. 151–170). Springer.

Paris, D. (2012). Culturally sustaining pedagogy: A needed change in stance, terminology, and practice. *Educational Researcher*, *41*(3), 93–97. doi.org/10.3102/0013189X12441244

Paris, D., & Alim, H. S. (Eds.). (2017). *Culturally sustaining pedagogies: Teaching and learning for justice in a changing world*. Teachers College Press.

Park, V., Groth, C., Bradley, J., & Rorrer, A. (2018). Reclaiming turnaround for equity and excellence: Leadership moves to build capacity for teaching and learning. In C. V. Meyers & M. J. Darwin (Eds.) *Learning disabilities and life stores* (pp. 17–28). Pearson.

Parker, K. N. (2022). *Literacy is liberation: Working toward justice through culturally relevant teaching*. Association for Supervision and Curriculum Development.

Pennebaker, J. W., & Smyth, J. M. (2016). *Opening up by writing it down: How expressive writing improves health and eases emotional pain*. (3rd ed.). The Guilford Press.

Perry, B. D. (2014). *Helping traumatized children: A brief overview for caregivers*. The Child Trauma Academy.

Peterson, S. (2019). Trauma-informed teachers and their perceived experiences with compassion fatigue. Publication No. 13900262. Doctoral dissertation, Capella University. ProQuest LLC.

Piaget, J. (1971). *Biology and knowledge*. Edinburgh Press.

Pianta, R. C. (1992). *The student–teacher relationship scale*. University of Virginia. education.virginia.edu/documents/ehdchild-parent-relationship-scale-short-form1992doc

Piazza, S. V., Rao, S., & Protacio, M. S. (2015). Converging recommendations for culturally responsive literacy practices: Students with learning disabilities, English language learners, and socioculturally diverse learners. *International Journal of Multicultural Education*, *17*(3), 1–8.

Pritchard, R. J. & Honeycutt, R. L. (2006). The process approach to writing instruction: Examining its effectiveness. In MacArthur, C. A., Graham, S. & Fitzgerald, J., Eds. *Handbook of writing research* (pp. 275–292). The Guilford Press.

Rainey, E. C. (2017). Disciplinary literacy in English language arts: Exploring the social and problem-based nature of literary reading and reasoning. *Reading Research Quarterly*, *52*, 53–71.

Ramirez, E., & Donovan, S. J. (2021). Harm and healing: Reading with an ABAR (anti-bias, antiracist) lens. *Voices from the Middle*, *28*(4), 54–59.

Ray, K. W. (2007). *Study driven: A framework for planning units of study in the writing workshop*. Heinemann.

Raymond, B. R. (2021). Creating a safe space for students to explore trauma and build resilience through young adult literature, creative composing, and personal experiences. In M. F. Rice & A. K. Dallacqua (Eds.), *Luminous literacies: Localized teaching and teacher education*, Emerald Publishing (pp. 71–83).

Rigell, A., & Banack, A. (2021). Dialogue as disruption: The power of middle grades classroom talk. In J. DeHart, C. K. Meyer, & K. Walker (Eds.), *Connecting theory and practice in middle school literacy* (p. 79–93). Routledge.

Rigell, A., Banack, A., Maples, A., Laugher, J., Broemmel, A., Vines, N., & Jordon, J. (2022). Overwhelming whiteness: A critical analysis of race in a scripted reading curriculum. *Journal of Curriculum Studies*. https//:doi.org/10.1080/00220272.2022.2030803

Rios, V. (2017). *Human targets: Schools, police, and the criminalization of Latino youth*. University of Chicago Press.

Robert Wood Johnson Foundation. (2017). Traumatic experiences widespread among U.S. youth, new data show. In Adverse Childhood Experiences: A RWJF Collection. rwjf.org/en/library/articles-and-news/2017/10/traumatic-experiences-widespread-among-u-s—youth—new-data-show.html#:~:text=Traumatic%20Experiences%20Widespread%20Among%20U.S.,or%20more%20Adverse%20Childhood%20Experiences

Rodríguez, R. J. (2019). *Teaching culturally sustaining and inclusive young adult literature: Critical perspectives and conversations*. Routledge.

Romero, V. E., Robertson, R., & Warner, A. (2018). *Building resilience in students impacted by adverse childhood experiences: A whole-staff approach*. Corwin.

Rosenblatt, L. M. (1994). *The reader, the text, the poem: The transactional theory of the literary work*. SIU Press.

Rumsey, A. D., & Milsom, A. (2019). Supporting school engagement and high school completion through trauma-informed school counseling. *Professional School Counseling, 22*(1), 1–10.

Rumsey, A. D., McCullough, R., & Chang, C. Y. (2020). Understanding the secondary exposure to trauma and professional quality of life of school counselors. *Professional School Counseling*, *24*(1), 1–11.

Salloum, S., Goddard, R., & Larsen, R. (2017). Social capital in schools: A conceptual and empirical analysis of the equity of its distribution and relation to academic development. *Teachers College Record*, *119*, 1–29.

Sanders, J., Munford, R., & Liebenberg, L. (2016). The role of teachers in building resilience of at risk youth. *International Journal of Educational Research*, *80*, 111–123.

Sanson, M., Strange, D., & Garry, M. (2019). Trigger warnings are trivially helpful at reducing negative affect, intrusive thoughts, and avoidance. *Clinical Psychological Science*, 7(4), 778–793.

Savitz, R. S., Roberts, L., & DeHart, J. (Eds.) (2023). *Teaching the "taboo": Diverse and inclusive literature is the way*. Routledge.

Savitz, R. S., Roberts, L. D., Jernigan, S., Ferrari, K., & Long, R. (2021). Young adult literature as a means for developing social awareness and supporting socio-emotional learning. In J. Tussey & L. Haas (Eds.), *Supporting social and emotional development through literacy education* (pp. 453–476). IGI Global.

Savitz, R. S., & Stockwell, D. (2021). Student voice is power: Incorporating critical witness and testimony in middle school classrooms. In J. Dehart., C. Meyer., & K. Walker (Eds.), *Connecting theory and practice in middle school literacy: Critical conversations*. Routledge.

Savitz, R. S., & Wallace, K. (2016). Using the inquiry process to motivate and engage all (including struggling) readers. *The Clearing House: A Journal of Educational Strategies, Issues and Ideas*, *89*(3), 91–96. doi: 10.1080/00098655.2016.1184923

Scales, P. C., Boat, A., & Pekel, K. (2020). *Defining and measuring social capital for young people: A practical review of the literature on resource-full relationships*. Report for the Bill & Melinda Gates Foundation. www.search-institute.org/wp-content/uploads/2020/05/SOCAP-Lit-Review.pdf?__hstc=75443661.133341ff5842f1d676304bcde57189c8.1625591380617.1633525264134.1633552629688.19&__hssc=75443661.1.1633552629688&__hsfp=2393683613

Serafini, F. (2001). *The reading workshop: Creating space for readers*. Heinemann.

Serravallo, J., & Goldberg, G. (2007). *Conferring with readers: Supporting each student's growth and independence*. Heinemann.

Shaull, R. (2000). Foreword. In P. Freire, *Pedagogy of the Oppressed* (pp. 29–34). Continuum.

Siebert, D., Draper, R. J., Barney, D. Broomhead, P., Grierson, S., Jensen, A., Nielson, J., Nokes, J., Shumway, S., & Wimmer, J. (2016). Characteristics of literacy instruction that support reform in content area classrooms. *Journal of Adolescent & Adult Literacy*. *60*(1), 25–33.

Siegel-Acevado, D. (2021). Writing can help us heal from trauma. *Harvard Business Review*. hbr.org/search?term=deborah%20siegel-acevedo

Sims Bishop, R. (1990). Mirrors, windows, and sliding glass doors. *Perspectives*, *6*(3), ix–xi.

Smagorinsky, P. (2019). *Teaching English by design: How to create and carry out instructional units* (2nd ed.). Heinemann.

Smith, J. M. (2019). Considerations for summer online book clubs. *The Reading Teacher*, *72*(5), 638–642.

Smith, D., Fisher, D., & Frey, N. (2015). *Better than carrots or sticks: Restorative practices for positive classroom management*. Association for Supervision and Curriculum Development.

Spencer, S. J., Steele, C. M., & Quinn, D. M. (1999). Stereotype threat and women's math performance. *Journal of Experimental Social Psychology*, *35*(1), 4–28.

Spires, H. A., Kerkhoff, S. N., & Medlock Paul, C. (2020). *Read, write, inquire: Disciplinary literacy in grades 6–12*. Teachers College Press.

Stedronsky, J., & Hawley Turner, K. (2020). Inquiry ignites! Pushing back against traditional literacy instruction. In J. Dyches, B. Sams, & A. S. Boyd (Eds.), *Acts of resistance: Subversive teaching in the English language arts classroom* (pp. 51–64). Myers Education Press.

Strauss, V. (February, 2022). This wave of book bans is different from earlier ones. *The Washington Post*. washingtonpost.com/education/2022/02/10/book-bans-maus-bluest-eye

Substance Abuse and Mental Health Services Administration. (2014). *SAMHSA's concept of trauma and guidance for a trauma-informed approach*. HHS

Publication No. (SMA) 14–4884. Substance Abuse and Mental Health Services Administration.

Sue, D. W., & Sue, D. (2008). *Counseling the culturally diverse: Theory and practice* (5th ed.). Wiley.

Taylor, L. A. (2020). Scaffolding literacy learning through talk: Stance as a pedagogical tool. *Journal of Adolescent & Adult Literacy, 74*(4), 375–383.

Tovani, C. (2021). *Why do I have to read this: Literacy strategies to engage our most reluctant students*. Stenhouse.

The Research and Evaluation Group. (2013). *Findings from the Philadelphia Urban ACE Survey*. Public Health Management Corporation. philadelphiaaces.org/philadelphia-ace-survey

Thorsborne, M. (2013). *Implementing restorative practices in schools: A practical guide to transforming school communities*. Jessica Kingsley Publishers.

Thorp, B. (February, 2016). *What does the academy value in a Black performance?* nytimes.com/2016/02/21/movies/what-does-the-academy-value-in-a-black-performance.html

Ticknor, A. S., Howard, C., & Overstreet, M. (2021). *It's not one more thing: Culturally responsive and affirming strategies in K–12 literacy classrooms*. Rowman & Littlefield.

Tsang, K. K. (2011). Emotional labor of teaching. *Educational Research, 2*(8), pp. 1312–1316.

Turner, K. H., & Reed, D. (2018). Responding to young adult literature through civic engagement. In J. S. Dail, S. Witte, & S. T. Bickmore (Eds.), *Toward a more visual literacy: Shifting the paradigm with digital tools and young adult literature* (pp. 41–52). Rowman & Littlefield.

Vasquez, M. V., Janks, H., & Comber, B. (2019). Critical literacy as a way of being and doing. *Language Arts, 96*(5), 300–311.

Vlach, S., & Burcie, J. (2010). Narratives of the struggling reader. *The Reading Teacher, 63*(6), 522–525.

Vygotsky, L. S. (1986). *Thought and language*. MIT Press.

Wesley, K. (2000). The ill effects of the five paragraph theme. *The English Journal, 90*(1), 57–60.Whitney, A. E., Blau, S., Bright, A., Cabe, R., Dewar, T., Levin, J., Macias, R. & Rogers, P. (2008). Beyond strategies: Teacher practice, writing process, and the influence of inquiry. *English Education, 40*(3), p. 201-30.

Wilhelm, J. D., Douglas, W., & Fry, S. W. (2014). *The activist learner: Inquiry, literacy, and service to make learning better*. Teachers College Press.

Windschitl, M. (2002). Framing constructivism in practice as the negotiation of dilemmas: An analysis of the conceptual, pedagogical, cultural, and political challenges facing teachers. *Review of Educational Research, 72*(2), 131–175.

Winn, M. T., Graham, H., & Renjitham Alfred, R. (2021). *Restorative justice in the English language arts classroom*. National Council of Teachers of English.

Winograd, K. (2003). The functions of teacher emotions: The good, the bad, and the ugly. *Teachers College Record, 105*(9),1641–1673.

Wright, R. (October, 1937). *Between laughter and tears: These low grounds*. unz.com/print/NewMasses-1937oct05-00022a02

Wroldsen, N. (2018). *Using restorative circles in schools*. Jessica Kingsley Publishers.

Yoon, B., Simpson, A., & Haag, C. (2010). Assimilation ideology: Critically examining underlying messages in multicultural literature. *Journal of Adolescent & Adult Literacy, 54*(2), 109–118.

Yurcaba, J. (August, 2022). A Florida school district added a parental "advisory notice" to over 100 books. *NBC News*. nbcnews.com/nbc-out/out-news/florida-school-district-added-parental-advisory-notice-100-books-rcna41779

Zacarian, D., & Soto, I. (2020). *Responsive schooling for culturally and linguistically diverse students*. W. W. Norton & Company.

Zembylas, M. (2005). Discursive practices, genealogies, and emotional rules: A poststructuralist view on emotion and identity in teaching. *Teaching and Teacher Education, 21*(8), 935–948.

Literature and Videos Cited

Ahmed, S. (2019). *Internment*. Little, Brown.

Alexander, M. (2020). *The new Jim Crow: Mass incarceration in the age of colorblindness*. The New Press.

Anderson, L. H. (2011). *Speak*. Square Fish.

Beyoncé. (n.d.). *Formation*. youtube.com/watch?v=WDZJPJV__bQ

Brubaker Bradley, K. (2020). *Fighting words*. Penguin Random House LLC.

Crowe, C. (2003). *Getting away with murder: The true story of the Emmett Till case*. Dial Books for Young Readers.

Derricotte, T. (1997). *Black boys play the classics*. University of Pittsburgh Press.

Diaz, A. (2019). *The crossroads*. Simon and Schuster.

Diaz, A. (2021). *Santiago's road home*. Simon and Schuster.

Evison, J. (2018). *Lawn boy*. Algonquin Books.

Fipps, L. (2021). *Starfish*. Nancy Paulsen Books.

Glasgow, K. (2018). *Girl in pieces*. Ember.

Glasgow, K. (2021). *You'd be home by now*. Delacorte Press.

Gratz, A. (2017). *Refugee*. Scholastic Press.

Hawthorne, N. (1988). *The scarlet letter*. Signet Classic.

Homer. (1919). *The odyssey*. Heinemann.

Hurston, Z. N. (2018). *Their eyes were watching God*. Virago Press.

Johnson, G. M. (2020). *All boys aren't blue: A memoir-manifesto*. Farrar, Straus, and Giroux.

Kobabe, M. (2019). *Gender queer: A memoir*. Oni Press.

Lee, H. (2006). *To kill a mockingbird*. Harper Perennial Modern Classics.

Lee White, G. (2023). *Dotson: My journey growing up transgender*. West Margin Press.

Magoon, K. (2015). *How it went down*. R. R. Donnelley & Sons Company.

May, J. (2016). *There are birds here*. Alice James Books.

Myers, W. D. (2009). *Monster*. Amistad.

O'Malley Cerra, K. (2016). *Just a drop of water*. Sky Pony.

Perez, A. H. (2015). *Out of darkness*. Carolrhoda Lab.

Pink, R. (2021). *Angel of Greenwood*. Feiwel and Friends.

Raleigh Baskin, N. (2016). *Nine, ten: A September 11 story*. Atheneum Books for Young Readers.

Rogers, T. (2014). *Eleven*. Alto Nido Press LLC.

Sánchez, E. L. (2017). *I am not your perfect Mexican daughter*. Knopf Books for Young Readers.
Sepetys, R. (2011). *Between shades of gray*. Philomel Books.
Sepetys, R. (2022). *I must betray you*. Philomel Books.
Shakespeare, W. (1998). *A midsummer night's dream*. Signet Classic.
Shakespeare, W. (1975). *Othello*. Clarendon Press.
Shakespeare, W. (2000). *Romeo and Juliet, 1597*. Oxford University Press.
Spinelli, J. (1999). *Maniac Magee*. Little, Brown Books for Young Readers.
Tarshis, L., & Egbert, C. (2021). *I survived the attacks of September 11, 2001: A graphic novel*. Graphix.
Thomas, A. (2017). *The hate u give*. Balzer and Bray.
Wiesel, E. (2006). *Night*. Hill and Wang.
Williams, T. (2009). *A streetcar named desire* (E. Browne, Ed.). Penguin Classics.
Winterson, J. (2018). *Oranges are not the only fruit*. Grove Press.
Woodson, J. (2018). *The day you begin*. Nancy Paulsen Books.

Index

About the Authors

Rachelle S. Savitz is an associate professor of reading/literacy at East Carolina University. She was previously a K–12 literacy coach/interventionist and high school reading teacher. She was the recipient of the 2020 Clemson Graduate Student Government Outstanding Graduate Student Advocate Award, the 2019 Association of Literacy Educators and Researchers' Jerry Johns Promising Researcher Award, and the 2018 Early Career Literacy Scholar Award from the American Reading Forum. Her research and work with teachers explore critical inquiry, culturally sustaining pedagogy, trauma-sensitive practices, and teacher self-efficacy related to disciplinary literacy and equitable literacy materials and curricula. She co-authored *Teaching Hope and Resilience for Students Experiencing Trauma: Creating Safe and Nurturing Classrooms for Learning* with Drs. Douglas Fisher and Nancy Frey and has publications in *Teaching and Teaching Education*, *Literacy Research and Instruction*, *Whiteness and Education*, and *Journal of Adolescent & Adult Literacy*.

Britnie Delinger Kane, PhD, is an associate professor of literacy education at The Citadel's Zucker Family School of Education. Her research interests focus on instructional coaching, as well as teachers' professional learning about how content-area and disciplinary literacy can support discipline-specific, conceptually rich, and equitable pedagogies, including current grant-funded research focuses on middle school mathematics teachers' use of literacy strategies to support culturally sustaining algebra instruction. Recent publications have appeared in *Teaching and Teacher Education*, the *Journal of Mathematics Teacher Education*, *Teachers College Record*, the *Journal of Teacher Education*, the *American Educational Research Journal*, the *Journal of the Learning Sciences*, and elsewhere.